CRIMINAL INVESTIGATIONS

CRIMINAL INVESTIGATIONS
A Scenario-Based Text for Police Recruits and Officers

James McAuliffe

Seminole Community College

Debbie J. Goodman

Series Editor

Upper Saddle River, New Jersey 07458

Library of Congress Cataloging-in-Publication Data

McAuliffe, James.
    Criminal investigations:a scenario-based text for police recruits and
officers / James McAuliffe.
     p. cm.
    Includes bibliographical references and index.
    ISBN 0-13-089580-6
     1. Criminal investigation—Handbooks, manuals, etc. I. Title.

HV8073 .M33 2002
363.25—dc21   00-069879

Publisher: Jeff Johnston
Senior Acquisitions Editor: Kim Davies
Production Editor: Lori Dalberg, Carlisle Publishers Services
Production Liaison: Barbara Marttine Cappuccio
Director of Production and Manufacturing: Bruce Johnson
Managing Editor: Mary Carnis
Manufacturing Buyer: Cathleen Petersen
Art Director: Marianne Frasco
Cover Design Coordinator: Miguel Ortiz
Cover Designer: Anthony Inciong
Marketing Manager: Ramona Sherman
Editorial Assistant: Sarah Holle
Interior Design and Composition: Carlisle Communications, Ltd.
Printing and Binding: Banta Harrisonburg

Prentice-Hall International (UK) Limited, *London*
Prentice-Hall of Australia Pty. Limited, *Sydney*
Prentice-Hall Canada Inc., *Toronto*
Prentice-Hall Hispanoamericana, S.A., *Mexico*
Prentice-Hall of India Private Limited, *New Delhi*
Prentice-Hall of Japan, Inc., *Tokyo*
Prentice-Hall Singapore Pte. Ltd.
Editora Prentice-Hall do Brasil, Ltda., *Rio de Janeiro*

10 9 8 7 6 5 4 3 2
ISBN 0-13-089580-6

In memory of
Mary Doris McAuliffe
She made the world a better place

CONTENTS

PREFACE

Criminal Investigations: A Scenario-Based Text for Police Recruits and Officers is designed to enhance the understanding of basic criminal investigations by use of real-life scenarios. It is geared towards the practical application of investigative tools, concepts, and protocols.

I wrote this text after having taught the subject for over nine years at the community college where I teach both academic and academy students and have found that, with slight modification, this basic investigation course material is suitable for both audiences.

ORIENTATION AND ORGANIZATION

The material in this book can be found in most texts on the subject as it is based upon general investigation concepts and practices that are taught across the nation. This text is different in that it takes a *proactive* approach to the learning experience.

Criminal Investigations: A Scenario-Based Text for Police Recruits and Officers involves the student directly by placing students into a scenario and then challenging the student to respond as if they were on the scene. This technique is based upon core principles of adult learning theory. Each chapter topic is reinforced with a quiz and a crossword puzzle for the student to complete.

This workbook has been field-tested in both academy and academic setting with great success. The last group of police academy students scored an average of 93 percent on a comprehensive final examination that was prepared outside the control of the author. Both groups of students reported that the text assisted them greatly in their understanding of the subject.

INSTRUCTOR MANUAL

The instructor's edition of the workbook includes a suggested syllabus and schedule for both academic and academy-based courses. It also provides answers to the scenario questions, quizzes, and crossword puzzles as well as suggestions for practical exercises and ideas on how to obtain materials for the exercises. A comprehensive midterm and final examination are also provided in this edition.

ACKNOWLEDGMENTS

I would first like to thank my wife Margit for her patience, understanding, and assistance during the writing of this text. This textbook would not have become a reality without the constant support and assistance of Kim Davies, Sara Holle, and Cheryl Adam from Prentice Hall, and Debbie Goodman from Metro Dade Community College. I would also like to thank Alexia Tlumacki, the Police Academy Classes and Criminal Justice academic students of Seminole Community College who field-tested the work.

INTRODUCTION

The purpose of this book is to assist the criminal justice student in conceptualizing *and* retaining the basic concepts of criminal investigation. In the past nine years, I have been teaching basic academy students as well as college students on this topic. I have found that all students studying investigations benefit from a scenario-based approach. This text incorporates real-world scenarios that allow students to relate to the subject matter with positive results.

After completing this book, the student will possess the tools that will assist them in effectively recalling key concepts for test purposes or for the demonstration of basic knowledge during an interview for a position in the field.

CRIMINAL INVESTIGATIONS

Preliminary and Follow-up Investigation Procedures

What is an investigation? Almost everyone has seen a television program depicting investigators attempting to solve cases involving murder and serious crimes. You may have developed a sense of what investigators do and maybe even how they go about doing it. If this *sense* is based upon most of the popular television shows, I would have to interject that you have more than likely been misled. In television, ratings demand entertainment. Observing action sequences involving the police kicking in doors at random and beating confessions out of suspects can be very entertaining. This is not, however, the way legitimate criminal investigations are conducted. In the real world these actions would result in:

- the termination of the officer's employment
- the arrest and conviction of the police involved in violating state law
- the removal of the officer's law enforcement certification

Name three more consequences:

- _____
- _____
- _____

Actual criminal investigation involves *making detailed and systematic inquiries and observations*. Criminal investigation is both an art *and* a science. Do you use a *system*? The first time you cut the lawn, it may have been pointed out to you by your father that the system you used didn't work. Large tufts of grass perhaps protruded in several areas of the newly cut lawn. Your system might have been to cut a little over here and a little over there until you were done. Because you didn't use a system, you missed some areas. Every time you go home you're more than likely to put your keys in the same location. This is a system you use so that you don't lose your keys. You *systematically* store your keys.

Have you ever lost your keys? How did you find them?

You (most probably) retraced your steps and *systematically* attempted to locate them. You may have interviewed possible witnesses and even a suspect (a family member who borrowed them) in an attempt to recover them. You conducted an investigation. If you think about it, you conduct investigations every day!

SCENARIO NUMBER ONE:
The Preliminary Investigation

You are a police officer. It is a nice Saturday morning about 11:00 A.M. The sun is shining and the birds are singing. You are in your patrol car riding in a neighborhood when you hear the sound of breaking glass and what could be best described as a heavy object striking something metallic. You begin looking for the source of the strange noise and come to 123 Oak Avenue. On the front lawn is a white Chevy with the hood up. On top of the roof of the vehicle is a man with a sledgehammer. The windshield has been smashed out, and the roof is dented and caved in from his weight. The man swings the sledgehammer and smashes out the back window. A number of tools are scattered around the ground and several empty beer cans litter the yard. The man appears to have been drinking. You stop your police car and get out. You ask him to get down off the car, and he extends his hand and points his middle finger upwards and announces that you should kiss his posterior. The kids standing across the street start laughing.

What are *you* going to do?

Identify five actions that you may take to "solve" this situation:

- _____

- _____

- _____

- _____

- _____

Before taking any of the above actions, you must conduct a *preliminary investigation*. The preliminary investigation determines *if the law has been broken and if it has been, what law specifically?* In the above example, no law has been broken. The owner of the vehicle was on his own property, and the vehicle belonged to him. He had been drinking and changing the water pump on his car when his ratchet wrench slipped for the third time, and for the third time he grated his knuckles down against the radiator. In his anger, he decided to beat up his car.

If the officer overreacts in this situation, he or she may face serious consequences.

Name three consequences that you may have experienced if you acted without first determining if a crime had been committed:

1. _____

2. _____

3. _____

In Order To Enforce The Law, You Must Know The Law!

SCENARIO NUMBER TWO:

Elements of the Preliminary Investigation

You are dispatched to a robbery at the local convenience store. The suspect is gone. No one was shot or beaten by the suspect. The victim is behind the counter, and a witness is seated on a milk crate by the soft drink dispenser. The overweight witness is sweating profusely and wiping his forehead with a handkerchief.

What is your first responsibility in this investigation?

_____

_____

Upon arrival at a suspected robbery, the officer should determine if the victim or anyone on the premise requires medical attention. This includes the witness who came into the store to buy a gallon of milk when the robbery went down. His profuse sweating and the fact that he is seated on a milk carton should draw your attention. The shock of being in the store during the robbery might be causing him a problem. He might even be having a heart attack. In determining if anyone needs medical attention, the officer investigating should look beyond the obvious. Just because no one is bleeding does not mean that the possibility of a life-threatening condition does not exist. If you overlook a possible medical emergency, you may very well place yourself and your department in a civil law suit for *failing to act.*

Police officers and corrections officers can be sued for things that they do—*or don't do.* If it can be determined that an officer knew, or *should have known* that a medical emergency existed and did nothing, he or she could be in serious legal trouble. If the officer deliberately failed to aid a person in need, Federal *criminal* charges could be brought against the officer for a civil rights violation. This is known as *deliberate indifference.* An inmate in a Florida jail died as the result of lack of medical attention. The nursing staff, corrections officers and a probation officer were held at fault and the county paid out over three million dollars in damages to the inmate's family. The officers in questions were lucky that they were only terminated from their positions and not arrested, prosecuted and setenced to prison.

During the preliminary investigation, the investigating officer must determine if a crime has been committed, and if so what crime? This may not be as obvious as one would think. (Remember the case of the man beating up his car?)

SCENARIO NUMBER THREE:
Elements of the Preliminary Investigation

You are dispatched to the local pawnshop. A man standing outside is extremely agitated. As you approach, he begins to yell and scream about his car being stolen. After you calm him down, he advises of the make and model of the car and when he last saw it.

What are you going to do first?

_____

_____

_____

Vehicles that are reported stolen in many cases are the result of repossession. The fact that the man was in front of a pawnshop could give you insight into the possibility of indebtedness and the likelihood of a lawful repossession by a creditor having taken place. You should inquire as to when he made his last payment on the vehicle and contact the dispatcher to determine if the creditor called in the repossession.

SCENARIO NUMBER FOUR:
Elements of the Preliminary Investigation

You are dispatched to a neighbor who complains of a bad smell coming from the house next door. Upon your arrival, you immediately smell a distinct foul odor that becomes stronger as you approach the house in question. As you look into the window, you observe a great number of flies on the inside of the glass. The neighbor has a spare key to the house. As you enter the house, you observe a man seated in the living room with an apparent gunshot wound to the head. The house has been ransacked.

What are you going to do first?

_____

_____

_____

The officer must preserve the integrity of the scene. This is accomplished by preventing anyone from accessing the scene who does not belong there. Family members and even some police officers who are not directly involved in the investigation are not permitted onto the scene. The person who discovered the body must be identified and his name and address along with proof of identity must be documented. *All* witnesses must be identified. The investigators will photograph the scene prior to any evidence being collected. The gun and any other evidence must be collected and the case properly documented on department forms. The offense report states the facts of the case and is usually prepared by the officer who initially responded to the scene. The officer will communicate with the dispatcher and supervisors. Part of this process may involve issuing bulletins for the arrest of an individual suspected of the crime or the suspect's description. The evidence from the case must be transported to the station after the scene has been processed. The evidence custodian will secure the evidence at the station in the evidence room.

Identify the responsibilities of the first officer at a crime scene:

1. _____

2. _____

3. _____

4. _____

5. _____

6. _____

7. _____

8. _____

What must the investigator determine during the preliminary investigation?

_____

_____

_____

What does the offense report contain, and who usually writes it?

_____

_____

_____

THE FOLLOW-UP INVESTIGATION

After the initial or preliminary investigation, the investigator reviews the information and evidence that has been collected. Fingerprints left at the scene by a suspect are known as *latent* prints. These fingerprints are deposited upon anything that the suspect has handled or touched and are made from the oil and perspiration which naturally occur on the skin of the fingers and hands. Latent fingerprints that were lifted from the crime scene might be compared with known criminals who have committed similar crimes in the past. If the fingerprint matches, it does not prove that the suspect committed the crime. It does place him or her at the scene and provides for further investigation to take place. The follow-up investigation involves gathering facts after the initial report and documentation of the case. The follow-up assists the investigator in establishing a case against a suspect.

What are the two major components of a follow-up investigation?

1. _____

2. _____

How do you know the suspect committed the crime? There are times when the investigator *knows* that a suspect committed the crime; however, he or she can't prove it. Many times this is the bulk of the investigation: proving that the bad guy did it! Although none of the methods explored here are completely foolproof, a combination of these methods could lead to a conviction in a court.

One way of proving that the suspect committed the act is by the suspect admitting that he or she did it. One of the methods of identifying the criminal suspect is by obtaining a **confession.** A confession is an admission of guilt that is freely given by a suspect. The confession could be made to a friend, acquaintance, cellmate, or to an investigator. It is not uncommon for a suspect to provide a *partial* admission to an investigator in order to better explain or minimize his or her exposure to blame for the crime.

If an eyewitness stated that he or she observed the suspect commit the crime, the case would be stronger. When the eyewitness identifies the suspect at a physical or photo line-up, the identification would be considered very solid and not as likely to be overturned.

If you add circumstantial evidence such as fingerprints left at the scene by the suspect, the case becomes even stronger as such evidence places the suspect at the scene. **Physical evidence** recovered from the suspects clothing such as blood from the victim would be difficult for the suspect to explain and certainly assists in the prosecution. Evidence is anything that helps prove or disprove a fact in question. *Proof is the result of evidence.* Physical evidence includes such things as fingerprints, bloodstains, fibers, weapons, or any physical thing that has value as evidence.

Informant information can lead an investigator to an unidentified suspect and in many cases begins the process of identifying the suspect. An informant is any person who comes forward to give the authorities information that helps solve a crime. An informant may have any number of reasons for providing information. Sometimes it is because he or she does not like the suspect and is seeking revenge upon the suspect, or the informant might feel that it is his or her civic duty to deliver the information. Whatever the motivation, informant information can be a major source of initial identification of an unknown suspect.

SCENARIO NUMBER FIVE:

Identifying the Suspect

You are the investigator assigned to missing persons. A woman has reported to you that her husband is missing. She relates that they had an argument, and he left her. You contact the missing person's employer, and he advises that he has not seen or heard from him. The employer relates that his desk has all of his personal effects, and it would have been out of character for him to leave like this. A woman who works at the topless bar with the wife of the missing man comes to the station and asks to speak to you about the case.

What questions would you ask this person?

_____

_____

_____

_____

The woman murdered her husband and then bragged to her friend about getting away with it. She was unaware that her friend was having an affair with her husband. As the result of her friend's testimony, the woman was successfully prosecuted for the murder of her husband.

Name the six methods of identifying a suspect:

1. _____

2. _____

3. _____

4. _____

5. _____

6. _____

Investigators use several procedures in a follow-up investigation. The first thing most investigators do is **review the offense report.** This consists of the investigator reading the written report and verifying all of the factual data contained in the report. The investigator will mentally go back to the scene and attempt to reconstruct the crime. This assists in developing leads. Part of this process requires the investigator to view all of the evidence and to make sure that requests for crime lab analysis have been properly submitted. If the evidence analysis request forms are not submitted, the evidence will sit on a shelf in the evidence room. There have been cases that were lost during the trial because substances were not chemically analyzed at the time of trial. In a cocaine possession case, the arresting officer used what is known as a presumptive field test to determine that the substance was probably cocaine. This test is sufficient for the development of *probable cause*. **Probable cause** consists of facts which lead an officer who is reasonably prudent, and based upon his or her education, training, and experience to believe that a crime has been or is in the process of being committed. Probable cause is required for *all* arrests. To win at trial, you must be able to prove *beyond a reasonable doubt*. **Beyond a reasonable doubt** is a standard of proof that the prosecutor must provide for a successful prosecution in a trial. In order to convict a person accused of a crime, the jury must find that the evidence presented provides proof that the accused committed the crime beyond a reasonable doubt. Defense attorneys attempt to defeat the prosecution by demonstrating that the standard has not been met. The failure of the officer to have an official chemical analysis from the crime lab at the time of trial caused two problems:

- the suspected cocaine was not analyzed by the higher standard of the crime lab and as a result was not admissible for evidence at the time of trial
- the failure of the officer to have the cocaine analyzed prior to trial cast serious doubt on the professionalism of the officer and his work

After ensuring that the evidence was properly sent to the crime lab, the investigator should **interview** and **re-interview** all witnesses including the reporting officer and victim. All interviews should be documented by audio or video tape recording.

The steps of an interview are:

1. The investigator turns on the recorder and identifies himself or herself, the case number, date, time, location, and the person being interviewed.
2. If the person is a suspect, the investigator will provide a Miranda warning.
3. The investigator will place the person being interviewed under oath in order to provide a record of sworn testimony.
4. Finally, the recording is transcribed into written form and signed by the person who was interviewed. This written record is enclosed in the case package and is presented to the prosecutor.

After having completed all of the interviews it is time to evaluate:

1. the statements
2. the evidence and reports from the crime lab

The investigator needs to constantly review the steps that he or she has taken in an effort to systematically cover all possibilities and then compare them to the probabilities.

SCENARIO NUMBER SIX:
Possibilities and Probabilities

You are the duty investigator. You are called to a scene where a man has been found seated in a car at the lake with a bullet wound in his chest. There was a typed suicide note on the dashboard of the car. You arrange for the note to be sent to the crime lab to attempt to recover any fingerprints. The crime scene technicians process the vehicle, and photograph and document the scene. The autopsy is scheduled for the following day. You interview the first responding officer to the scene and any witnesses who were present when the body was found.

What is your major concern as an investigator in this case of apparent suicide?

_____

_____

_____

When you review the report from the crime lab, you discover that the fingerprints on the note do not match those taken from the dead man. The autopsy report revealed that the man was already dead at the time of the gunshot wound. The gunshot was *postmortem*. Postmortem is Latin for after death. The cause of death was strangulation. Two latent fingerprints were recovered from the neck of the dead man. An informant called in to report that the dead man's business partner had commented that he killed his partner after unsuccessfully attempting to buy him out of the business. Fingerprints from the partner were found on the note and later were identified as being the same as those recovered from the neck of the dead man. You have the suspect come down to the station for an interview. After you advise him of his rights and place him under oath, you show him the evidence, and the dead man's partner confesses to the murder.

In the above case, the suspect was identified, located, and arrested. He was interviewed in custody and confessed to the crime. The typewriter that was used to write the note was located at the suspect's apartment and entered into evidence. The typewriter was later identified as the same used to generate the letter based upon the unique typeset characteristics. In cases where a suspect is involved in burglary or robbery, a search of his or her residence may reveal stolen property that could be recovered.

In some cases, the investigator should consider electronic surveillance or the possible use of a lie detector such as the polygraph or voice stress analyzer. In cases of internal theft, electronic surveillance and lie detectors can be great tools if they are used properly.

In all cases, it is imperative that the investigator is in contact with the prosecutor. The prosecutor cannot do his or her job without the complete cooperation of the investigator. Most problems with a case can be worked out prior to going to trial. For example, if an investigator forgot to send the evidence to the crime lab and the trial is next week, the prosecutor could ask for a continuance and get extra time so that the lab could analyze the material. The investigator who comes to court ready for trial and never told the prosecutor that he or she failed to send the evidence for analysis can expect to be on his or her own. The prosecutor may even join in with the judge and defense counsel in attempting to discover what went wrong, and in doing so, further discredit the shabby investigator.

DISCUSSION QUESTIONS

Identify five procedures an investigator uses in a follow-up investigation:

1. _____

2. _____

3. _____

4. _____

5. _____

What is the difference between **probable cause** *and* **beyond a reasonable doubt** *in a criminal case?*

_____

_____

_____

Explain what could happen if an investigator does not pay attention to detail or is careless in his or her work.

_____

_____

SUMMARY

We discussed the preliminary and follow-up investigation procedures. We defined **investigation** as: **making detailed and systematic inquiries and or observations.** The **purpose** of a preliminary investigation is to establish whether a criminal act has been committed and, if so, what type. The key elements of a preliminary investigation are: request medical aid, if necessary; determine if a crime has been committed, and if so, what type; preserve the integrity of the crime scene; identify witnesses; document case and gather evidence; prepare an offense report stating facts; issue bulletins; and transport evidence.

The **follow-up investigation** involves gathering information subsequent to the initial report to establish a case.

Methods of identifying criminal suspects include: confessions, witness testimony, circumstantial evidence, physical evidence, informant information, and line-up identification (physical and photo).

Procedures for conducting a follow-up investigation include: reviewing the offense report to develop leads; viewing all evidence and ensuring proper submission to the crime laboratory; conducting interviews with the reporting officer, victim, and any witnesses; evaluating statements, evidence, and laboratory results; considering surveillance and polygraph examinations; identifying, locating, and arresting the suspect; conducting in-custody interviews; recovering stolen property if applicable; and communicating with the prosecutor's office.

Attention to detail is one of the most crucial duties of the investigator. If the investigator is sloppy or inattentive, the case will be lost in court regardless of the quality of the evidence.

CROSSWORD PUZZLE

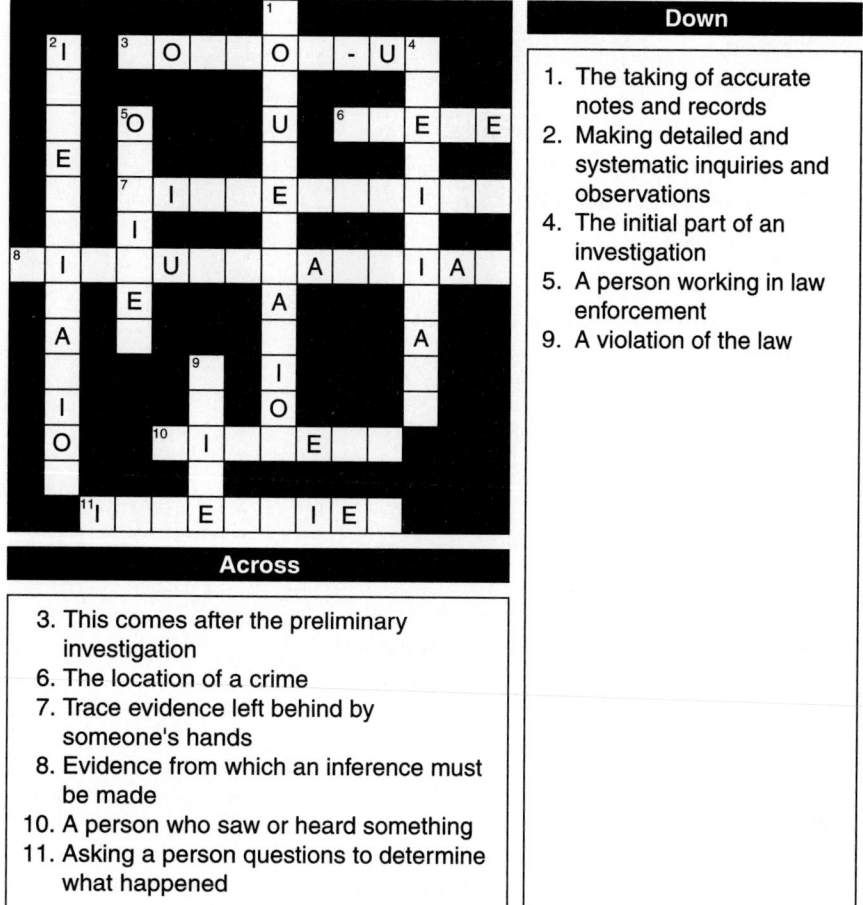

Down

1. The taking of accurate notes and records
2. Making detailed and systematic inquiries and observations
4. The initial part of an investigation
5. A person working in law enforcement
9. A violation of the law

Across

3. This comes after the preliminary investigation
6. The location of a crime
7. Trace evidence left behind by someone's hands
8. Evidence from which an inference must be made
10. A person who saw or heard something
11. Asking a person questions to determine what happened

Test Your Knowledge

For each multiple choice question select the best possible answer.

1. An investigation is best described as:
   a. an art.
   b. a science.
   c. as both an art and a science.
   d. neither an art nor a science.

2. The making of detailed and systematic inquiries and observations is know as:
   a. an inquiry.
   b. an inquest.
   c. an investigation.
   d. dedicated research.

3. The preliminary investigation determines:
   a. if the law has been broken.
   b. specifically what law has been broken.
   c. who you take to jail.
   d. a and b.

4. The first priority of the responding officer at the crime scene is:
   a. to render first aid.
   b. dust for fingerprints.
   c. secure the scene.
   d. all of the above.

5. Witnesses at a crime scene must:
   a. be allowed freedom of movement.
   b. be identified.
   c. be allowed to leave.
   d. be allowed to communicate between themselves.

6. The offense report is usually prepared by:
   a. the rookie.
   b. the sergeant.
   c. the investigator.
   d. the initial responding officer.

7. All of the following are examples of procedures used in a follow-up investigation except:
   a. lifting prints at the scene.
   b. interviewing officers who responded to the scene.
   c. comparing evidence from the scene to suspects.
   d. establishing a case against the suspect.

8. Requests for crime lab analysis are made by:
   a. the patrol officer.
   b. the forensic analyst.
   c. the investigator.
   d. the crime scene tech.

9. The burden of proof at a criminal trial is:
   a. a preponderance of the evidence.
   b. probable cause.
   c. the opinion of the judge.
   d. beyond a reasonable doubt.

10. An investigator who is careless is likely to:
    a. have his or her cases suppressed and thrown out of court.
    b. lose credibility.
    c. be reprimanded or held in contempt by the court.
    d. all of the above.

Crime Scene Search Procedures

Before you can search a crime scene, there are some preliminary issues at hand. The first thing is to get to the crime scene quickly and safely. In order to accomplish this, you have to know: (1) where you are, (2) where you need to go, and (3) the best route to take. This may sound simple, but given the nature of the call and amount of stress you are experiencing, this may be difficult, especially if you are new!

When you first become employed as a law enforcement officer, you are put into a field training program. Part of this program involves learning the layout of streets and the best routes to take when responding to calls. A law enforcement officer must know where he or she is and be able to articulate this at all times. It is customary in most departments that officers respond on the radio by stating their identification number and location when called. Knowing where you are and having a virtual map of your environment in your head is imperative for a law enforcement officer to be effective. In the beginning, this may seem like an impossible task, given the size of the area and number of highways, streets, roads, and alleyways. After a while, you become more comfortable as you gain knowledge of the streets and the best routes to take. Now you must factor in the *time of day!* The best route on midnight shift may not be the best route during the day. Just because it is the most direct, does not mean that it is the *quickest.* Traffic patterns, railroads, and other obstacles that may not be apparent at first, can raise their ugly heads in the midst of your response to a serious crime and either delay or prevent your timely arrival.

SCENARIO NUMBER ONE:

Responding to the Call

It's Friday evening at 5:15 P.M. You just received a dispatch that a silent robbery alarm has been activated at Joe's bar. You are at 25th Street, one block away from the main road that runs through town. Joe's bar is on 1st and Oak. Oak Avenue is two blocks east of the main road. The most direct path is down the main road.

What is the best route to this possible robbery? How would you respond (lights, siren, etc.)?

_____

_____

_____

*What decisions must you make **immediately**?*

_____

_____

_____

Everyone has witnessed a police officer racing down the road with lights and siren blaring. Sometimes this is not the best method to respond to a crime scene. If the officer does not want to alert the criminal that he or she is coming, then the lights and siren may not be the desired method of approach. A quick response obeying the traffic control devices and speed limits can be very effective. Having lights and sirens does not give the police officer the right to drive in a reckless manner. Many officers have lost their jobs and careers because of foolish actions involving speeding to a scene. If you were to wreck your car on the way to an officer calling for help, what good would you be? You would actually have compounded the situation. Now other officers have to come to your assistance, and this reduces the number of officers who would have responded to the officer in need of assistance.

Identify four factors that affect an officer's ability to respond to a crime scene:

1. _____

2. _____

3. _____

4. _____

Name three problems that can arise from an officer responding to a crime scene in a reckless manner:

1. _____

2. _____

3. _____

Once you have arrived in the area of the crime scene, you must decide where you will park and how you will approach. This is potentially dangerous and depends upon the nature of the call. Once you have arrived on the scene, it is imperative that you render first aid if it is necessary. Ask the people at the scene if they are in need of medical attention. In many cases, people who are in shock from an incident such as a significant criminal offense are reluctant to speak up. It is *your* responsibility to determine who needs medical assistance.

If you arrive at the scene and are able to identify the suspect, then you should apprehend the suspect. This may involve your approaching and handcuffing the suspect, or conducting a further investigation by interviewing the suspect while your back-up officer arrives. If there is no need to rush, then it is usually wise to make arrests with multiple officers present. This provides a safety net for you in two ways: A suspect is less likely to physically resist multiple officers, and if allegations of unlawful conduct are made against you by the suspect, you have witnesses who can testify on your behalf.

How big is a crime scene? This is one of the questions that you will be required to make upon arrival at the scene. You must determine the extent of the crime scene. Size depends upon the type of crime and location of the incident. Some scenes are small, and others are extremely large. It is usually wise to overestimate the size of a scene rather than underestimate. It is impossible to increase the area of the scene once people have been allowed to enter and contaminate it. Once you make your decision and mark off the scene, it is generally too late to make it larger as people tend to walk all around the marked-off area attempting to see what's going on.

There is an old adage in crime scene investigation, "Everyone who enters brings something into the scene, and everyone who leaves takes something out of the scene." One of your most important duties is to *protect and preserve* the crime scene. Protect it from curious onlookers and relatives and protect it from co-workers, the media, and anyone who has no business entering. Now common sense needs to prevail. If the police chief wants to enter the scene, it would be professional suicide to attempt to prohibit him or her from entry. You must, however, enter the chief's name, rank, and time of entry and exit on the *contamination list*. The contamination list is the formal documentation of all persons entering and leaving the crime scene. This list of names becomes a part of the case report, and all persons listed are subject to subpoena. The list alone prevents most officers from entering out of curiosity.

Communication in law enforcement is extremely important. This is why each officer carries a radio and is in the constant and immediate reach of dispatchers, other officers, and supervisors. During an incident, the dispatchers must be able to keep everyone informed of your status and the status of the scene. You must communicate the situation to your agency and update this information regularly. You will find that if you have been dispatched to a serious event, you will be inundated with requests for information from everyone above you in rank. This can be frustrating at times, and you must remember that the people who are asking for updates are genuinely concerned for your well-being. You must give them information on injuries, number and identity or description of suspects, suspect vehicles, direction of travel, and any other pertinent information.

Witnesses are human beings and, as such, will attempt to remove themselves from harm's way. You must understand this when you encounter resistance from eyewitnesses who do not want to be involved. Remember that the eyewitness has most probably observed a violent act perpetrated upon a person, and he or she does not want to be next! This is especially true in a correctional setting. Witnesses will try to leave the scene and go home or anywhere other than the crime scene. You must retain your witnesses. It is extremely important that you do not let them leave. Sometimes a suspect may be found among the witnesses. When a crime occurs in a jail or prison, the perpetrator is always present. Sometimes a witness can identify the suspect by name. Witnesses will not give you information unless you ask. So ask! Sometimes you must be firm with witnesses. Even if they become hostile, you must not let them leave until you have obtained the appropriate information from them. This includes identification, telephone numbers, addresses, etc., so that they can be contacted at a later date. You may even have to arrest a witness. This would be a last resort and only used in unique circumstances such as an extremely hostile witness. In a correctional setting or even in some high-crime areas, the witness does not want to appear to be cooperative in front of his or her peers.

SCENARIO NUMBER TWO:

The Witness

You are a corrections officer in a state prison. An inmate has just been stabbed in the yard. While he is being taken to the medical unit, you observe one of your informants standing in the group of inmates where the offense took place. As you approach him, he becomes loud and abusive. He calls you a racial slur and tries to walk away. You call for a back-up officer, and you begin to struggle with him. When the other officer arrives, the inmate is pinned on the ground, handcuffed, and taken into confinement. Once in custody and away from the other inmates, he provides the name of the person who did the offense and where the shank (homemade knife) can be found.

Why did the inmate become abusive and need to be locked down?

_____

_____

Arresting him or taking him into custody allows him to demonstrate appropriate resistance to law enforcement and provide the information away from the scene.

Once the scene is secured, you should begin to record the events in chronological order. The notes you take must be usable to generate the formal police report. It is important to be thorough in your observations. Always note lighting conditions and visibility as they often come up at trial in the cross-examination of witnesses.

Identify the eight responsibilities of the first responding officer at a crime scene:

1. _____

2. _____

3. _____

4. _____

5. _____

6. _____

7. _____

8. _____

After the scene is secured, the scene will be *searched*. A crime scene search is planned and coordinated. In order for the search to be of any value, it must be legal. The purpose of searching a crime scene is to locate physical evidence involved in the crime and witnesses who can testify as to the occurrence. The first priority in preparing for the crime scene search involves viewing the entire scene and determining what you are looking for and how to locate it. How many people will you need to accomplish the search? Will you need any special equipment or resources such as K-9 or air support? This process is known as surveying the crime scene.

Once you have determined how you are going to accomplish the search, it is time to start the documentation process. This includes recording the scene by photographs and sketches. Photographs must be taken prior to anything being moved or disturbed. A photograph must be a true and accurate portrayal of the scene as it was at the time it was taken. A sketch must be able to stand up in court regardless of how rough it might be. Thorough and accurate documentation of a crime scene is crucial to any criminal case.

Part of the documentation process involves locating any and all evidence. When a piece of evidence is located, it must be photographed and sketched. In the sketch, measurements are made from a fixed object to the piece of evidence so that it can be placed in a spatial relationship on the sketch. The knife was three feet, two inches from the corner of the living room and seven feet, five inches from the front door. The sketch allows the investigator to recreate the scene later in an accurate fashion. All physical evidence must be located by measurement and documented.

Fingerprints are everywhere. Finding fingerprints is easy. It's finding the *right* prints that may be a little tricky. Fingerprints are worthless unless they provide a connection between the suspect and the crime. Your car has just been broken into and your stereo was stolen. Fingerprints of a suspect were found on the left-front fender of your car. These fingerprints place the suspect in the area but do not prove anything. He could say he was walking in the parking lot, stumbled, and placed his hand on your car to steady himself. If his fingerprint was found inside your car and he had no legitimate explanation for his print being in your car, then you could infer that he committed the crime. Fingerprints are invisible for the most part and at a crime scene you must search for prints. They could be anywhere.

SCENARIO NUMBER THREE:
The Fingerprint

You are the duty investigator and have been called out to an apartment where the body of woman has been discovered. Her nude body is located on the floor next to the bed. A pair of pantyhose is tied tightly around her neck. Her tongue is protruding and has turned black on the end. As you gather statements of other tenants of the apartment, you discover that she was a single woman who lived alone. While walking through the apartment you notice that the toilet seat is in the up position.

What is the significance of this observation?

_____

_____

_____

_____

Females normally use the toilet with the seat down. As a matter of fact, they tend to get upset with men when they leave the seat up (which results in a rude awakening for women in the middle of the night). The careless murderer in this case left his fingerprints on the seat as he raised it to urinate. People are creatures of habit.

What problems might occur if an investigator handled evidence at a crime scene prior to photographing it?

_____

_____

_____

_____

Why should a "rough" sketch be able to stand up in court by itself?

_____

_____

_____

_____

How could a "perfect" fingerprint be absolutely worthless to an investigator?

_____

_____

_____

_____

Evidence can take many forms. An investigator must determine what evidence should be collected first and what evidence can wait to be collected. This determination is based upon the nature of the evidence. A gun, for example, is not going to disappear if it begins to rain. Blood evidence, on the other hand is a different story. The more fragile the evidence, the greater the urgency of its collection.

A crime can take place anywhere. A person can get robbed on a street corner, in a house, on a boat or a train. There are only three types of crime scenes possible: 1) outdoor 2) indoor 3) conveyance. The *outdoor* crime scene takes place anywhere outside. The *indoor* crime scene is obviously inside. The *conveyance* crime scene takes place on any vehicle, vessel, or plane.

There are seven major considerations in the search process. These are consistent issues that must be dealt with at most crime scenes.

1. *The protection of the crime scene is first and foremost.* If the scene has not been protected, then you can assume that it has been contaminated. Once a scene is contaminated, any evidence that you gather is contestable in court. Could someone have placed the evidence in the crime scene? How many people had access to the area? As discussed earlier, before you can start to search a crime scene, you have to determine how big it is.

2. *Determine the boundaries of the crime scene.* Once this is accomplished, you can set up your crime scene tape or post officers strategically to ensure that nothing enters the scene. If the scene were in a cow pasture, would you allow the cows to walk all over and destroy your evidence?

3. *Decide how exactly are you going to search.* There are five basic types of search patterns. You must choose a search pattern and then create an action plan for implementation. In an extremely small crime scene, it may only take one or two people to accomplish the task. On large crime scenes, it could take hundreds. Assistance from organizations such as the military or the Boy Scouts could be very beneficial in certain cases. Boy Scouts should never be used if the object of the search is most probably deceased. Common sense must rule. It would be unfortunate if the sight of a putrefied corpse traumatized one or more of the Boy Scouts. It would also result in a sizable lawsuit for the department, extremely bad press, and professional suicide for the investigator in charge.

4. *Proper instruction and coordination of personnel* involved in the process of searching must be accomplished at both the initial briefing and then modified once the search commences. The manner in which the investigator addresses the personnel is crucial.

5. *The investigator must coordinate the search.* The investigator is in charge of a crime scene and has authority to issue directives in relation to the scene and the investigation. However, an investigator who acts superior, demanding, and rude, will not get the assistance he or she needs to accomplish the desired goal. The officers who are delegated to assist will "cop an attitude," and their participation could be one of walking around and not actually searching. The investigator is asking for assistance, not demanding compliance. If the officers and participants view themselves as members of the team and believe that the task at hand is important, then the results will inevitably be more positive. Most searches do not involve a missing child, and the investigator has to motivate the searchers during the search.

6. After a predetermined time, *the search must be concluded.* Termination of the search is linked to the type of crime and associated cost factors. In the search for a missing child, the search may very well last days. In the search for a weapon or other evidence, the search may last only a few hours. This is especially true if the investigator is using the assistance of officers who are taken off their normal patrol functions for the search or are on overtime status. This brings us to documentation.

7. *Documentation of the search is the final step.* There is an old adage in law enforcement: "If you didn't write it down, then it didn't happen." All things pertinent to a case must be recorded, including attempts to locate evidence. This documentation also provides justification for overtime

and other related costs for administration, as well as lost productivity for officers involved in the search. When an officer is assigned to searching a crime scene, he or she is not answering calls or enforcing traffic, and this will reflect on his or her daily or monthly statistics. Contrary to popular belief, quotas are not imposed upon police officers. This is not to say that if an officer does nothing all day or month that he or she won't hear from the sergeant. There is an *expected productivity level* from each officer based upon where and when they are working as well as their particular assignment.

Name the three types of crime scenes.

　　1. _____

　　2. _____

　　3. _____

What are three problems that could occur if a crime scene were not protected?

　　1. _____

　　2. _____

　　3. _____

What could happen to a search if the investigator in charge were viewed as being rude, demanding, and acting superior towards the officers assigned?

_____

_____

_____

_____

Name three reasons why a crime scene search must be properly documented.

　　1. _____

　　2. _____

　　3. _____

As mentioned earlier, there are five basic search patterns. The first pattern is the **strip** or **line search.** This is one of the most simple to accomplish. The military uses this every day to ensure there is no litter on the ground or in the training areas. On selected mornings, all of the personnel who live in the barracks are required to fall out and line up in what is known in the army as "police" call. This is done in order to "police" up the area. A long line is formed, and the area is cleaned of cigarette butts or any litter that is visible. By lining up in this fashion it is impossible to overlook any trash. This same technique is used to collect spent brass on the firing line in recruit academies across the country. It is also used commonly by police to search for small items such as a discarded weapon in a field or for a missing child in the fields or open areas where the child was last seen.

Strip or Line Search

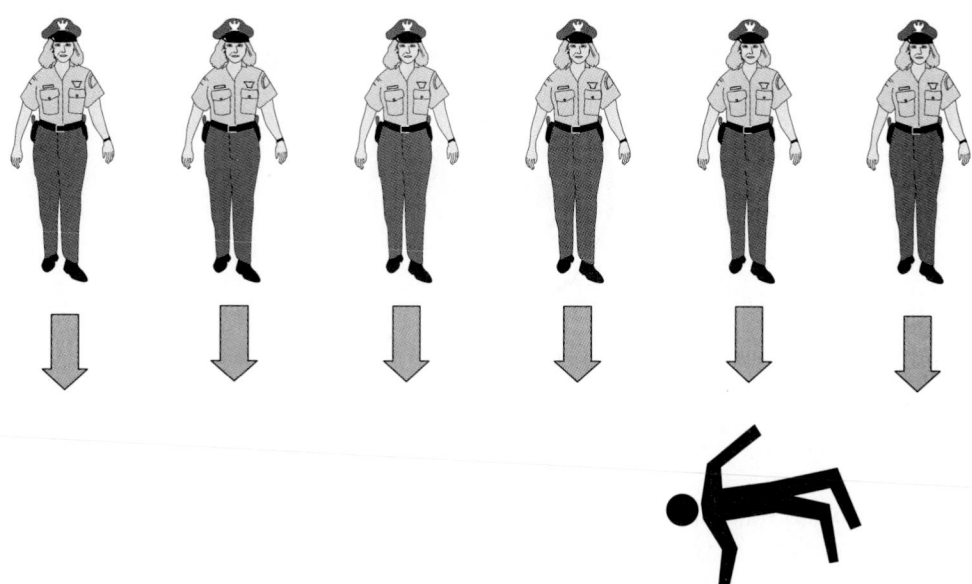

The line search is probably the most common of all types of searches. It is simple to conduct and relatively easy to supervise. It is used to cover large areas of ground, and is one of the best uses of a large group of searchers.

The next type of search pattern is the **grid search.** Archeologists do this type of search regularly when they are digging for artifacts. Sets of string lines are placed over the area to be searched. This forms a series of boxes. Each line is labeled and identifies exactly where the artifact is recovered. The grid is normally used for smaller areas where the investigator is searching for small evidence.

Grid Search

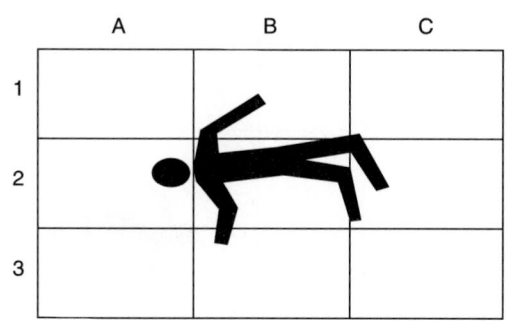

The next pattern is the **spiral search pattern.** This type of search involves a person walking in a spiral and can be accomplished by starting in the center and spiraling out or beginning on the outside and spiraling in. The goal is to cover the area completely.

Spiral Search

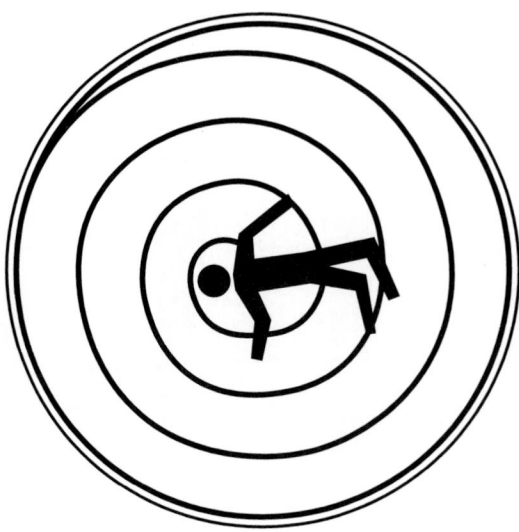

The spiral search can be used in many different areas. If you were alone and wanted to search your backyard for your keys or something small, this method would ensure that you covered every square foot. You would start on the outside perimeter of your yard and work around until you were in the center. It is one method for singular searchers to ensure that they have covered the entire scene.

The **quadrant or zone search** is a combination search technique. In this pattern, an area is divided up into zones. Each zone or sector is assigned to a person or team. The person or team then decides what type of pattern they will use to search the zone. They may use a line, grid, or spiral search in their zone, whichever is best suited.

Quadrant or Zone Search

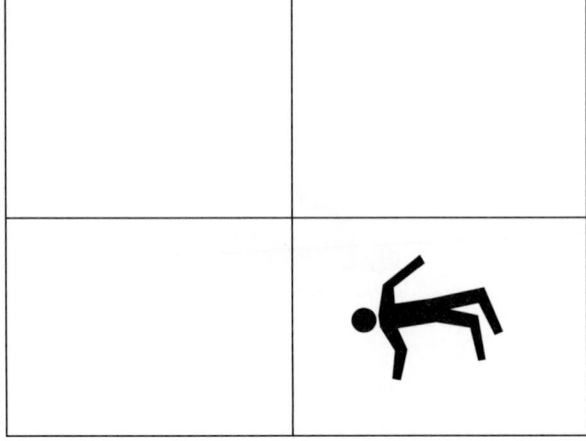

Wheel or Pie Search

The final type of search pattern is known as the **wheel** or **pie search pattern.** This search is mostly used for searching vast areas by airplane. It is used a great deal by the coast guard when they search for people lost at sea. It is usually accomplished by determining a central point. This point may be the last known place that the object of the search was known to be. Once the point is determined then an aircraft will fly to that point and radiate out from that point. The plane will fly out in a wheel formation and constantly return to the center point until a wheel is completed.

SCENARIO NUMBER FOUR:
The Crime Scene

You are the first responding officer. A woman was discovered in her house on Oak Avenue by her landscaper. She was found on the floor and had been sexually battered, physically beaten, bound, and gagged. You arrived at the same time as the paramedics who removed her from the scene via ambulance.

On the following page, you will find a diagram. The house at 103 Oak Avenue is the home of the above victim. Follow the directions on the diagram and then respond to the following questions:

1. How did you decide upon the size of the crime scene?

_____

_____

2. What search pattern did you choose? Why?

_____

_____

3. What assistance did you request?

_____

_____

4. Where did you place the vehicles and tape? Why?

_____

_____

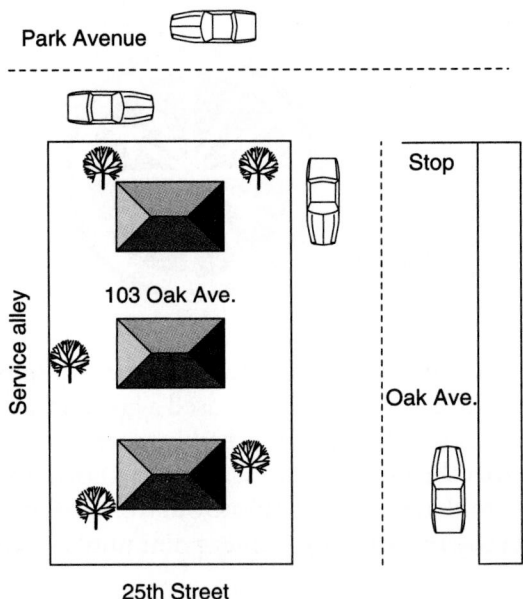

1. *Determine the extent of the crime scene and mark it off with crime scene tape:*

_____

_____

2. *Identify where you would post officers and vehicles:*

_____

_____

3. *Identify the areas to be searched:*

_____

_____

What type of search would you use to find a lost child in a large wooded area? Why?

_____

_____

_____

_____

What type of search would you perform on a shallow grave? Why?

_____

_____

_____

Identify two major considerations in conducting a search:

1. _____

2. _____

What type of search would not be best suited for the use of volunteers such as the Boy Scouts?

_____

_____

SUMMARY

We discussed the duties and responsibilities of the first responding officer in relation to a crime scene. We began with the initial crime scene response issues and concluded with types of search patterns.

The responsibilities of the first responding officer at the scene include: Arriving quickly but safely; rendering first aid; apprehending suspect(s); determining the extent of crime scene; protecting and preserving the scene; communicating with agency; retaining witnesses and suspects, and recording the events.

The definition of a crime scene search is: a planned and coordinated legal search of a crime scene to locate physical evidence and witnesses to the crime under investigation.

The steps of a crime scene search include: surveying the crime scene, recording the scene by photographs and sketches, documenting all physical evidence, and searching for prints.

Evidence that is of a fragile nature must be gathered first.

The types of crime scenes are: indoor, outdoors, and conveyance.

The seven major considerations involving crime scene searches are:

protection of scene, boundary determination, choice of search pattern, instruction of personnel, coordination of personnel, termination of search, and documentation.

The methods of searching a crime scene include: strip or line search pattern, grid search pattern, spiral search pattern, quadrant or zone search pattern, and the pie or wheel search pattern.

The thorough search of the crime scene is a crucial component of an investigation.

An investigator usually gets one shot at recovering evidence from a crime scene.

CROSSWORD PUZZLE

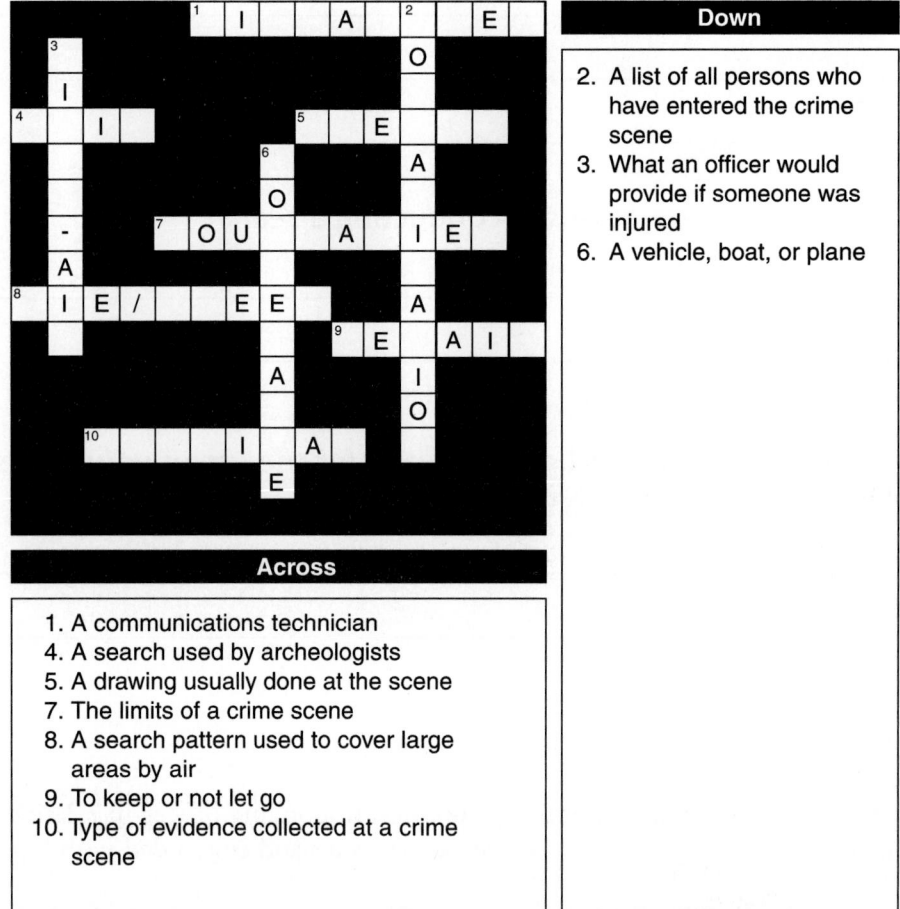

Down

2. A list of all persons who have entered the crime scene
3. What an officer would provide if someone was injured
6. A vehicle, boat, or plane

Across

1. A communications technician
4. A search used by archeologists
5. A drawing usually done at the scene
7. The limits of a crime scene
8. A search pattern used to cover large areas by air
9. To keep or not let go
10. Type of evidence collected at a crime scene

Test Your Knowledge

For each multiple choice question select the best possible answer.

1. All of the following are examples of the responsibility of the first responding officer to a crime scene except:
   a. lifting prints.
   b. arriving quickly but safely.
   c. apprehending the suspect.
   d. recording the events.

2. A planned and coordinated legal search of a crime scene to locate physical evidence and witnesses to the crime under investigations is known as:
   a. a grid search.
   b. a wheel search.
   c. a line search.
   d. a crime scene search.

3. A record of all persons who entered a crime scene is known as:
   a. a crime scene record.
   b. a crime scene tally sheet.
   c. an evidence list.
   d. a contamination list.

4. The first step in a crime scene search is:
   a. searching for prints.
   b. surveying the crime scene.
   c. recording the crime scene by photographs and sketches.
   d. all of the above.

5. At a crime scene which evidence type would be collected first?
   a. a hammer used in a murder
   b. semen found at the scene
   c. blood found at the scene
   d. b and c above

6. All of the following are examples of crime scenes except:
   a. outdoor.
   b. inside.
   c. conveyance.
   d. indoor.

7. In protecting a crime scene:
   a. the officer prohibits unauthorized people from entering.
   b. the officer can prohibit the chief from entering.
   c. the officer records who enters on the contamination list.
   d. a and c.

8. In determining a crime scene boundary:
   a. it is better to go smaller than bigger.
   b. it is better to go bigger than smaller.
   c. scenes should be no larger than a roll of crime scene tape.
   d. none of the above.

9. A search pattern that is best used to search small areas and is frequently used in archeological digs is known as:
   a. line search.
   b. spiral search.
   c. quadrant search.
   d. none of the above.

10. A search pattern that is used to search large areas of land or sea and is frequently used by air search teams is known as:
    a. a grid search.
    b. a pie or wheel search.
    c. a quadrant or zone search.
    d. a spiral search.

Crime Scene Drawing and Diagramming

Diagramming is one method of recording an event. In law enforcement, there are numerous reasons for preparing a diagram.

SCENARIO NUMBER ONE:

The Crash Scene

You are working as a patrol officer. You are dispatched to a traffic crash. Upon arrival, you observe a yellow four-door passenger car, and a blue two-door sport utility vehicle, both of which are inoperable in the middle of the intersection. You determine that the drivers are not injured and first aid is not required. A back-up unit arrived and is assisting with traffic control. You and the other officer are routing traffic away from the crash. You request two tow trucks to remove the vehicles. As this is a major road, traffic is backed up about two miles. The sergeant is on the radio asking why it's taking so long to clear the roadway. The tow trucks arrive and hook the vehicles. You advise the sergeant that they are in the process of being towed. The vehicles are pulled into a large parking lot across from the scene, and the roadway is cleared and traffic is now moving. The driver of the blue car advises that the driver of the yellow car violated her right of way. The driver of the yellow car claims that the driver of the blue car is at fault.

Now that all of the commotion has stopped and the pressure to move the vehicles has subsided, you start to reconstruct the scene. Was the yellow car facing the curb on the right or left side the blue car? Or was that the blue car? There is damage on the front and sides of both vehicles. This isn't a simple rear-end collision that can be identified by the front of one vehicle crashing into the rear of another. The answer to this problem lies in the positioning of vehicles on the roadway. So much was going on when you arrived, that you didn't really pay attention to the position of the vehicles. Now *you* have a problem.

What should the officer have done at the above scene to prevent this type of problem?

_____

_____

Can the officer rely on the testimony of the drivers?

_____

How can the officer determine who is at fault?

_____

Who is directly responsible for the accurate reporting and documentation of this vehicle crash?

_____

How likely is a crash report to be used in court?

_____

To avoid the above problem, officers responding to crash scenes or any scene for that matter will create a "rough sketch" of the scene, which will aid in them remembering location of vehicles for the "formal diagram." The rough sketch is made upon arrival as soon as possible and prior to the vehicles being moved and includes location, direction, and measurements. The most common type of sketch is known as the "bird's eye view" looking down on the scene from above. Normally this is done on a clipboard or a note pad from the officer's pocket.

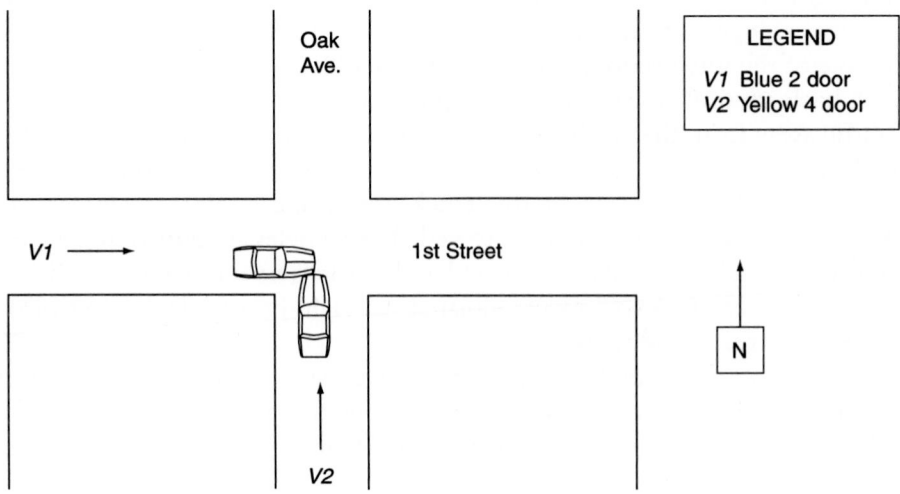

A rough sketch should contain an overview of the scene as it was at the time the officer arrived. A rough sketch must be able to **stand-alone** in court. The formal crash diagram is produced on a form that is specific for the purpose.

Although the crash scene is probably the most common of diagrams that a police officer makes, there are basically four other situations that call for diagrams. They are:

1. crime scene
2. report writing
3. evacuation
4. planning diagrams

SCENARIO NUMBER TWO:

The Crime Scene

It's Thursday night at 11:00 P.M. You are on routine patrol in your zone. Dispatch activates a tone, which alerts you that a serious call is about to be given. The location is in your zone, and you are dispatched to a domestic dispute involving a firearm. Upon your arrival at the house, a female is sitting on the front steps rocking back and forth. She tells you that she killed her husband and that she wasn't going to take it any more. Your back-up arrives, and you secure the woman in his car. You enter the house and observe a middle-aged male with an apparent gunshot wound to the head. He is dead. The murder weapon is on the kitchen table next to the phone.

As the first responding officer to a crime scene, you have certain responsibilities.

Identify five of your responsibilities as the first responding officer to this crime scene:

1. _____

2. _____

3. _____

4. _____

5. _____

As a police officer, one of your many duties is to be able to recall and accurately testify as to what you observed upon arrival at a scene. A sketch of the scene and notes that you took shortly after securing the suspect would be helpful. You documented the spontaneous confession that the suspect made in your notes as well as the weather and light conditions, didn't you? Of course you did! Your sketch of the scene detailed the location of the body, the gun on the table, and anything else of significance. Once you secured the scene, you initiated the contamination list and documented the investigators, crime scene technicians, and other personnel as they entered and exited the scene.

Another reason for preparing a sketch is to describe in a **written report** the location of items found or evidence discovered. Sketches such as these are tools that are used to further explain, describe, or inform the reader of the report. Remember that the person who reads the report was not at the scene, and the purpose of the document is to inform or describe how the scene appeared at the time you arrived. What may seem inconsequential at the time of writing may have great relevance to the reader.

In emergency situations such as an **evacuation** of a large number of citizens from an area, a diagram of the evacuation route is an absolute necessity. The posting of officers along the route and traffic flow issues can be discussed and evaluated by the use of diagrams. When any major event is planned, a diagram is drawn. In the execution of a search warrant or raid, a poorly drawn diagram could put officers' lives in danger. Poorly drawn or incomplete diagrams could also spell disaster in providing security at a public event like the Daytona 500 or for a visiting dignitary like the president of the United States appearing at a fundraiser.

Name three problems that could occur if a diagram is improperly prepared:

1. _____

2. _____

3. _____

One of the first issues that a person wishing to draw a diagram encounters is equipment. The diagram must be neat, accurate, legible, and it must make sense to the reader. A pencil or pen can be used to draw the scene. Some people like the flexibility of a pencil and the ability to erase mistakes. A pen provides a more permanent document. Graph paper enables an officer to draw more accurately, as do a ruler and compass. A tape measure is an absolute necessity. In order to obtain accurate measurements, a steel tape is preferred, as fiberglass tape tends to stretch. In a courtroom, this tiny stretch can cause accuracy issues to become an issue. If an officer wishes to make a "scale" drawing, he or she must be absolutely positive of calculations. A scale drawing is made in major cases such as those involving homicide. Most of these diagrams are computer-generated for accuracy. Like a scale model, everything must be an exact reproduction of the scene reduced in a presentation. An error in conversion can cause a diagram to be impeached. It is safer to present diagrams in which you note "not to scale" on the diagram when not sure or confident. A template is a tool that is used to draw items that are repetitively applied to diagrams such as cars in a crash diagram. It is usually made of plastic and has punch-outs of various crime scene or traffic items. Most agencies use computerized drawing programs for major crime scenes. Even traffic enforcement officers have laptop computers with all of the major intersections in their jurisdictions indexed. Each intersection is a template, and all the officer has to do is to "drag and drop" the vehicles in place. As the law enforcement community depends more and more upon computers, there will be less need for paper forms, reports, and "hard copies." Modern police agencies issue laptops to each officer as a standard part of their equipment. At the end of their shift, officers turn in their reports in the form of floppy discs or up-link directly to the supervisors' computer.

WHY DIAGRAM?

The diagram that you make creates a permanent record of the scene as you saw it. It is easier to show a diagram to someone than try to explain the scene verbally. You can show the distances between items, which can be very important. A diagram can reconstruct a crime scene or crash site for people who have vested interests in the event. Insurance companies for example, are very interested in crash information. A diagram helps explain and clarify what is written in a report and what is seen in photographs or other forms of documentation.

THE FORMAL DIAGRAM

This is the diagram that is presented in court. On the formal diagram the investigator should be identified by name, rank, and identification number. The date that the diagram was made, case number, and type of case should also be on the diagram as well as the exact location of the scene. Symbols are used instead of writing out what is being identified in the diagram. This is done to save space. For example, the letter A may be used to identify a weapon such as a knife. In the legend, the word knife would follow the letter A. A legend identifying the symbols is usually contained in a box and is displayed on the diagram. The scale of the diagram must be identified, and if the diagram is not to scale this must be noted. In the diagram, all major items of evidence must be identified and measurements presented which place the evidence in proper spatial relationship to one another and the location in general.

SURVEYING

Surveying is the method of measuring distances from fixed objects in order to place evidence at a scene in proper spatial relation to the scene. There are three basic methods:

1. **Triangulation.** This method involves measuring from two fixed points to the evidence and forms a triangle. Numerous triangle-shaped measurements could be made in a diagram.

2. **Rectangular Coordinate.** This method involves measuring from two fixed points that are perpendicular to the evidence and forms a right angle.

3. **Straight Line.** This method simply involves measuring from two fixed points that are on either side of the evidence in a straight line.

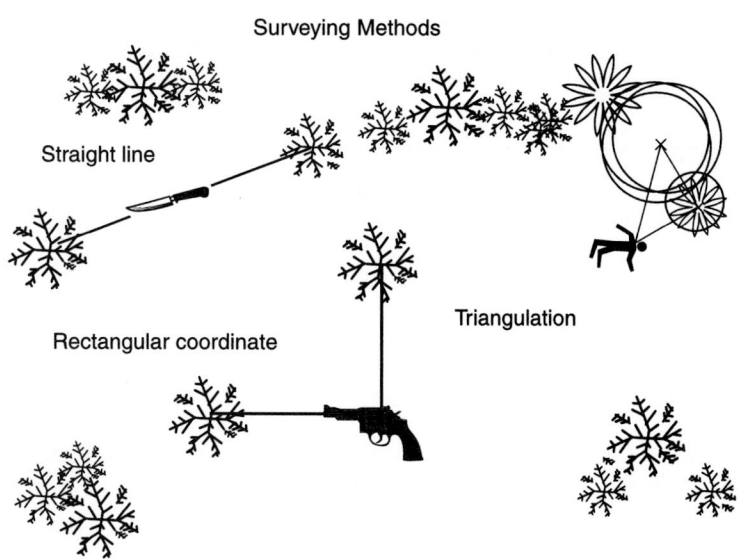

Surveying Methods

Straight line

Rectangular coordinate

Triangulation

Regardless of the method, accurately measuring the location of the evidence is crucial. A crime scene diagram should produce information from which the scene could be accurately recreated. This is frequently done in courtrooms to explain to the jury such things as distance between items.

The selection of the type of surveying method depends upon the scene and what is available to the investigator. For example, on an indoor scene, fixed objects such as room corners or doorframes could be used. In an exterior scene, corners of buildings or trees could be used for the fixed point. It should be noted that a vehicle couldn't be used as a fixed point as it can be moved. In the case of vehicle crashes, spray paint is used to mark the location of vehicles on the roadway. This enables the investigator to revisit the scene after the vehicles are moved if necessary.

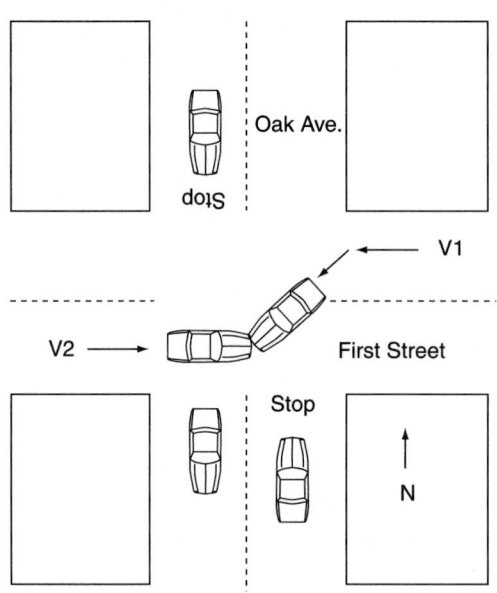

Which vehicle is at fault in this crash? Why?

_____

_____

_____

SCENARIO NUMBER THREE:
The Crime Scene

You are the investigator on the scene of an apparent homicide. You must document the scene by creating a diagram. The homicide took place in the family room of a house in an upscale neighborhood. The victim is a male who was shot in the chest. His body was on the floor in front of the sofa. A

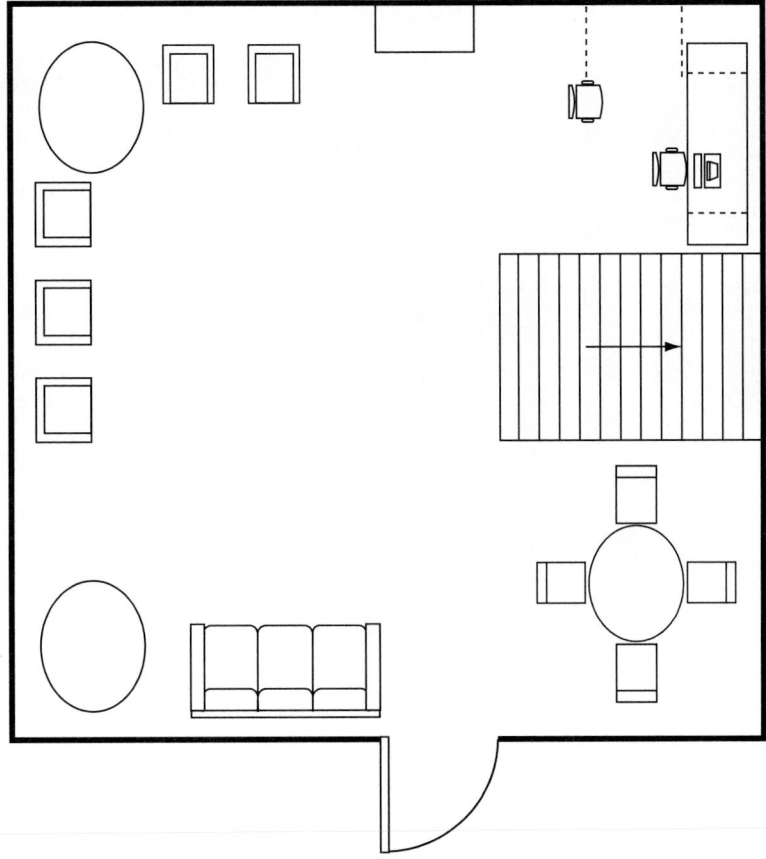

weapon (presumed to be the murder weapon) was found on the floor by the stairs. There are bloody footprints (barefoot) on the stairs going up and on the floor around the body. There is a pool of blood under the body and on the sofa. Draw the evidence into the crime scene on the following page. Make sure to include all of the necessary information and diagram requirements.

SUMMARY

In this chapter, we discussed the circumstances in which diagramming is used such as accidents, crime scenes, report writing, evacuations, and planning. We reviewed the materials used in the construction of a diagram and the importance of diagramming. We also identified the basic attributes of a rough diagram and presented an example. We defined surveying and presented the most common methods of surveying with examples of each. In this chapter, you were provided with the opportunity to complete a crime scene diagram. The crime scene diagram must stand-alone in court. If it is done well, it allows the jury to experience the scene, as it was when you were there. Done poorly, it is an opportunity for a defense attorney to have a field day.

CROSSWORD PUZZLE

Down

1. One of the most common events diagramed
2. A method for recording an event
3. A method of measurement that places the evidence between two points
4. The relationship between items measured at a crime scene
5. Sworn statements given in court
6. What a rough sketch must do in court
8. The best measuring tapes are made from this
9. Another name for executing a search warrant

Across

7. A method of measurement that forms triangles
10. The viewpoint of a diagram

Test Your Knowledge

For each multiple choice question select the best possible answer.

1. Circumstances in which diagramming is used include all of the following except:
   a. accident scenes.
   b. writing a traffic citation.
   c. report writing.
   d. crime scene.

2. Planning is one area that involves using diagramming. All of the following are examples of planning except:
   a. public events.
   b. security measures.
   c. responding to an accident scene.
   d. raids.

3. Measurements are crucial to accurate documentation. What type of tape measure is best to use at a crime scene?
   a. fiberglass
   b. plastic
   c. steel
   d. none of the above

4. A diagram that is properly made:
   a. replaces notes and photographs.
   b. provides a temporary record of conditions.
   c. aids in the reconstruction of a crime scene.
   d. hinders in reconstruction of an accident.

5. All of the following information must be included in a formal diagram except:
   a. supervisor's name and rank.
   b. investigator's name and rank.
   c. case number.
   d. address of the scene.

6. A _____ is used to identify the symbols that represent objects or points of interest on the sketch.
   a. ledger
   b. legend
   c. legion
   d. none of the above

7. The basic attributes of a rough diagram or sketch include:
   a. usually drawn at the station.
   b. must be complete enough to stand alone.
   c. does not require measurements.
   d. will not be used in court so is not important.

8. The _____ sketch is the most common method of diagramming
   a. cat's eye view
   b. dog's eye view
   c. bird's eye view
   d. squirrel's eye view

9. Types of surveying include:
   a. triangulation.
   b. rectangular coordinate.
   c. straight line.
   d. all of the above.

10. The type of surveying technique which locates objects by their distance from two perpendicular lines is know as:
    a. triangulation.
    b. rectangular coordinate.
    c. straight line.
    d. none of the above.

CHAPTER 4

Crime Scene Photography Techniques

Crime scene photography has been around since the advent of the camera. There are photographs on record from the 1800s of crimes that had taken place. One example is a series of photographs of the unsolved serial killings that took place in England. The name given to the perpetrator was "Jack the Ripper," and the case was never solved. Interest still remains high in this case, and numerous recent documentaries discussed this and other notorious cases. The photographic evidence remains in a condition that could be used in court today. In a murder case, there is no statute of limitation. On occasion, you will see a case from years ago being tried. Nazi war criminals are still sought and prosecuted based upon testimony and photographic evidence that is over fifty years old.

Photography is an extremely valuable tool. In a courtroom, the jury can be transported back in time to the scene as it was, through the use of proper photographic documentation. They can get an accurate understanding of the unique and specific circumstances that were present at a scene when the police arrived. They can see what the police saw. The old adage "a picture is worth a thousand words" seems as true today as it ever was. Photographic evidence provides an indefinite record of a crime scene. This record can be accessed indefinitely to assist the investigator in revisiting the scene or in presenting at trial the scene to a jury.

SCENARIO NUMBER ONE:
The Old Case

In 1962, a murder occurred. A woman was found in her apartment strangled to death. No one was arrested. In 1998, her former boyfriend bragged to a friend that he had killed her and gotten away with it. He told his friend that he strangled her with a cord from her bathrobe. The murder weapon (cord) was never disclosed to the media. He told him this while he was drunk. The suspect's friend called the police and reported his story. The police activated the old investigation. The original investigator had long since retired, and the investigator assigned to this old homicide was born four years after the crime was committed.

Can a crime that was committed this long ago be successfully prosecuted?

_____

_____

_____

All of the photographs taken at the scene were in black and white. Can they be used in court? What would concern you about them?

_____

_____

_____

What should the jury be able to understand from the photographs presented to them during the trial? Why?

_____

_____

_____

Do you think the murderer would be convicted on the evidence presented? Why or why not?

_____

_____

_____

There are legal considerations in the presentation of any evidence. Photographic evidence is no exception. In order for photographic evidence to be admitted in court, it must be material or relevant to the case at hand. In other words, photographs of a suspect's personal lifestyle, that have nothing to do with the crime, will not be admitted into evidence. The photographs must not appeal to the emotions or tend to prejudice the jury. They must be free from distortion and must present an accurate representation of the scene, as it was the day it was taken.

SCENARIO NUMBER TWO:

The Relevant Photographs

A man is arrested at his apartment for computer fraud. He had used the Internet to bilk thousands of dollars out of people. During the search of his apartment, a large collection of homosexual pornography was discovered. This pornography was of adult males and not illegal by statute. During the search, photographs were taken of the suspect, the suspect's apartment, and all evidence involved in the case. When the search warrant for the suspect's apartment was served, the suspect was home and refused to answer the door. Fearing that evidence would be lost, the officers broke the door and entered the apartment. Upon entering the apartment, they found the suspect wearing a woman's wig, bra, panties, and a garter belt with stockings and high heels. Photographs were also taken of his pornography collection.

You are the Judge

What photographs would you allow into evidence?

_____

_____

What photographs would you not allow in court? Why?

_____

_____

_____

Do you think that the entry by police was appropriate? Why or why not?

_____

_____

_____

SCENARIO NUMBER THREE:

The True and Accurate Representation

You are the first responding officer to a possible homicide. The investigators and the crime scene technicians have not arrived yet. One of your fellow officers is assisting in maintaining the perimeter. Inside the house is a victim of a gunshot wound. A semi-automatic pistol is on the floor next to the body. You are positioned at the front door. Your fellow officer enters and returns with the suspected murder weapon in his hand. He tells you that he unloaded the weapon to make it safe. You advise him that picking up the gun was a mistake, and he states that he will just put it back and no one will know the difference.

What is your responsibility in this matter?

_____

_____

What are you going to do when the investigators get to the scene?

_____

_____

How could this incident affect the case?

_____

_____

_____

Photographs of a crime scene must be taken *prior* to anything being moved or examined. Once a piece of evidence has been moved, it can never be placed *exactly* where it originally was. Is this a big deal? Yes, it is! The scene must be documented properly, and it is impossible to testify *under oath* that the scene presented in the photographs is a true and accurate representation of the scene as it was when the officers arrived. Once anything is moved, the photograph taken after the fact must be explained. This explanation will give a defense attorney all he or she needs to attack the procedures at the crime scene. This could result in each and every piece of evidence being questioned and scrutinized more than necessary. Defense attorneys constantly search for flaws in a case that will give the jury "reasonable doubt." Once this is established, the case is all but over. Poor evidence-collection techniques and documentation procedures are on the top of the list of the defense attorney attempting to discredit the police and create reasonable doubt in the minds of the jury.

Police officers responding to a homicide scene must secure the scene prior to processing it. This includes such things as marking off the area with crime scene tape and not allowing unauthorized personnel into the scene. Once the scene is secured, the investigators begin the documentation process. The first phase of documentation involves photographing the location of the offense. The first photographs taken are known as the *establishing shots*. These crucial photographs initiate the photographic evidence process by establishing the location of the scene. The establishing photographs are taken a distance from the scene and may include such things as the name of the apartment complex, the apartment cluster within the complex, and then the front door of the apartment. As with all crime scene photography, the initial sequence of photos are taken from a distance and continue as the focus of the photographs narrows on to the object. This process repeats itself until the crime scene technician is focusing on minute trace evidence inside the scene.

Overlapping photographs must be taken to ensure that the entire scene has been captured.

SCENARIO NUMBER FOUR:

The Establishing Shots

You are the crime scene technician who has been dispatched to the Harvey Frolic Arms in reference to a homicide in apartment B3. After you survey the scene, your first duty is to begin photographing the scene.

What photograph are you going to take first? Why?

_____

_____

The sequence of photographs at a crime scene is extremely important. This sequence would occur as follows:

1. The first photograph is of the front of the apartment complex focusing on the large sign in front of the rental office which states "Harvey Frolic Arms, If you lived here you'd be home now." In this photograph, you have the name of the complex and the street address on the glass door of the rental office along with after-hour phone numbers.
2. The next photograph is of the building identified by a large "B" on the corner.
3. The next photograph is of the front door of the scene that has a "B3" on it.
4. The next photographs would be of the view from the front door as it is opened, the hallway, the entrance to the living room where the body is, and then several photographs of the body from different angles around the room.

5. The final photographs would be close-ups of the body and evidence. Once again, the evidence would be photographed from a distance and then closed in on.

Investigators also take photographs of witnesses and add them to the case file. This is done to refresh the memory of the investigator as to who can testify to what.

SCENARIO NUMBER FIVE:

The Missing Photographs

You are the investigator who has been assigned to a probable homicide. As the investigator, you are responsible for all that pertains to the investigation. This includes all documentation and security of the scene. The victim in this case has been discovered next to a dumpster behind the Wal-Mart Plaza. Two homeless men discovered the body while they were looking for treasure in the garbage. Patrol has taped off the alleyway behind the store and retained the two homeless men for you to interview. The victim was stabbed to death. A large smear of blood is on the side of the building across from the dumpster and a knife covered with blood is on the ground beneath it.

What photographs need to be taken first? Why?

_____

_____

_____

Describe the sequence of photographs that the crime scene technician should have taken:

_____

_____

_____

_____

A patrol officer picked up the knife after the photographs were taken. He advised that he put it right back exactly where it was. Do you anticipate any problems with this? Why?

_____

_____

_____

The crime scene technician advised that she took all of the photographs of the scene prior to your arrival and that the scene is now ready to be processed by fingerprinting and recovering evidence. When you get the photographs from the lab, you notice that *no establishing shots were taken.* There were plenty of photographs of the knife, and the dumpster, but none of the overall location.

What kind of problem do you foresee in court because of this?

_____

_____

_____

What would you do to remedy the situation?

_____

_____

_____

In crime scene photography, it is important to be able to identify evidence in a photograph. A **marker** is used to accomplish this. Markers call attention to objects in a scene and allow the person who is looking at the photograph to more fully understand what he or she is looking at. A marker could be a small traffic-like cone that has a number on it or a small flag similar to what cable companies use to mark underground cables. You may have seen the police on television marking shell casings in a shooting scene with small numbered cones.

Once the object has been marked in a photograph it has our attention. Now a question that may come to mind is size. In a photograph, it is difficult to determine the size of the object or distance between two objects. If the object has been enlarged, the viewer needs to know the amount of enlargement. This is done through the use of **measuring devices.** Rulers and stick-on-tape measures are routinely used to demonstrate size. In some instances, these measuring devices can be used to call attention to minute evidence such as blood spatter. In some old crime scene photography, a dime was placed in the photograph to demonstrate relative size.

There is more to crime scene photography than just taking pictures. Even if you are an accomplished photographer and are very good, the laws of evidence apply to photographs taken at a crime scene, and all necessary documentation must be made. This includes making a report including the case number, negative film file number, and photographer's name. Also included in the report is the subject, location, time and date, light source, distance from subject, type of camera and lens, type of film, shutter speed, and lens setting. Even the height of the camera from the ground needs to be in this report. If there are photographs of witnesses on the roll, their names must be noted. Additional remarks about the case conclude your report. A crime scene photographer must be able to demonstrate knowledge of photography in the court. For example, you are on the witness stand and are not able to recall the lens you used or the film speed or make of camera that you operated on the day in question. The defense attorney will have an easy time demonstrating that you do not know what you are doing and that anything that you produced is questionable at best. With all of this information in your report, it would be a simple matter to refresh your memory and provide the appropriate responses.

PROPER PROCEDURES FOR CRIME SCENE PHOTOGRAPHY

Once the scene is secured, the photographs must be taken prior to anything being moved or disturbed. Medical personnel take priority when they must check on a victim and perform any medical procedures necessary. Once they have accomplished their mission, the crime scene may be photographed. In cases where a victim is transported to the hospital, it is obvious that the crime scene is photographed without the victim being present. In this circumstance, it is understood that medical personnel out of necessity have moved items.

When photographing a scene, a tripod should be used if possible. This provides the photographer with a consistent distance from the ground as well as a steady camera that is not subject to movement caused by some unpleasantness present at the scene. When photographing evidence in the scene, relative size must be presented through the use of measuring devices. The photographs of the crime scene should be devoid of people other than the victim. Photographs of other officers walking through and looking at evidence detract from the purpose of the photograph and bring questions as to the movement of evidence prior to photographing. If the officers are moving around while you are photographing then one could conclude that they are contaminating the scene and the photographs taken are not an accurate representation of the scene as it was prior to being disturbed. At the conclusion of the photographic recording of the scene, the record of the process must be completed. The log must match the photographs taken. There is no room for personal photographs of officers at the scene. Imagine if you took a photograph of a co-worker and then left it out of the roll. The sequence of photographs would not match, as a photo would be missing. A defense attorney would have a field day with this information, and once again the focus of the trial would shift from his or her client to the police and their procedures.

SUMMARY

In this chapter, we discussed the importance of photography in law enforcement. Photography is a valuable tool. It allows the jury to obtain an accurate understanding of specific situations, can be stored indefinitely, and provides the investigator with a visual record of the scene. Some legal considerations of admissibility that must be taken into consideration include materiality and relevance of the objects photographed, emotional or prejudicial photographs, and distorted photographs that do not represent the scene accurately. Photographs must be taken prior to any detailed examination of the scene to provide an accurate representation of the scene undisturbed. We discussed the types of photographs and the difference between markers and measuring devices. We also described information that should be required to identify photographs taken at a crime scene. And, finally, we reviewed the proper procedures for photographing a crime scene.

CROSSWORD PUZZLE

Down

1. The device used to collect photographic evidence
2. Evidence that must be a true and accurate representation of the scene
4. A professional who has technical expertise
6. Other than the victim, these should not be in crime scene photographs

Across

2. By following these, you can't go wrong
3. The initial photographs taken at a crime scene
5. A device on which a camera is mounted
7. Out of focus or not clear
8. This requires a log which identifies individual frames
9. An object used to point out evidence at a crime scene

Test Your Knowledge

For each multiple choice question select the best possible answer.

1. All of the following are reasons why photography is a valuable tool except:
   a. provides the investigator with a visual record of the crime scene.
   b. allows the court and jury to obtain an accurate understanding of specific situations.
   c. photographic evidence may not be stored indefinitely.
   d. both a and b above.

2. Some photographs may not be allowed in court. This is because they:
   a. are not relevant to the issue.
   b. are distorted and do not represent the scene.
   c. will prejudice the jury.
   d. all of the above.

3. Providing a true and accurate representation of the scene undisturbed is accomplished by taking the photographs:
   a. prior to the detailed examination of the scene.
   b. before the paramedics mess it up.
   c. after the captain and lieutenants leave.
   d. after it has been processed for fingerprints.

4. The first photograph taken at a crime scene is known as:
   a. the first one.
   b. the establishing shot.
   c. the big shot.
   d. the front door.

5. Types of photographs taken at a crime scene include all of the following except:
   a. witnesses.
   b. officers.
   c. evidence.
   d. location.

6. _____ help in identification, call attention to particular objects and enable a viewer to more fully understand the scene or object represented.
   a. measuring devices
   b. pointers
   c. markers
   d. stamps

7. _____ show relative size, distance between objects, the degree of enlargement, and call attention to particular trace evidence.
   a. Measuring devices
   b. Pointers
   c. Markers
   d. Stamps

8. Types of markers include:
   a. measuring tape.
   b. small traffic cones.
   c. small flags.
   d. b and c.

9. Types of measuring devices include:
   a. rulers and measuring tapes.
   b. cones.
   c. flags.
   d. b and c.

10. All of the following is information used to properly identify crime scene photographs except:
    a. name of the photographer.
    b. type of camera.
    c. name of the Chief of Police.
    d. time and date.

Lifting Latent Prints and Fingerprinting

The importance of fingerprints in law enforcement cannot be overstated. Fingerprint evidence has been responsible for countless convictions and is one of the most used forensic crime scene processing tools utilized to date.

SCENARIO NUMBER ONE:

The Vehicle Burglary

After reading this paragraph, you decide to drive to the store. You go to your vehicle and notice that the glass has been smashed in and your brand new CD player is missing along with a case containing twenty-five CDs. You call the police and report a vehicle burglary and grand theft. The police arrive, and the officer obtains all of the pertinent information for her report. She then proceeds to the trunk of her patrol car and recovers what appears to be a fishing tackle box. Inside the box are a number of brushes and some canisters of different-colored powders. Also, you notice a number of rolls of what appears to be wide scotch tape and blank white and black cards. The officer removes one of the brushes, dips it into a canister of dust, shakes off the excess and begins to lightly dust the door of the car. As she is dusting, fingerprints that were not visible before appear. It is apparent that the fine powder sticks to something left on the surface of the door from someone's fingers. After she develops the prints she unrolls scotch tape and carefully places it on top of the print. She slowly peels the tape off and places it on a card. The print is no longer on the door. After writing her name, ID, case number, and print recovery location on the card she places it in her folder. The officer repeats

49

this same procedure at different locations on the outside and the inside of the vehicle. Just before she leaves the scene, she gives you her business card with the case number and advises that an investigator will be in touch within the next couple of days.

IF YOU WERE THE INVESTIGATOR IN THIS CASE, THEN . . .

1. *Of what value are the fingerprints lifted on the exterior of the vehicle to your investigation?*

_____

_____

_____

2. *What can you determine from the fingerprints taken on the inside of the vehicle?*

_____

_____

_____

3. *What alibi could a burglar use in explaining his or her fingerprint being found on the outside of the vehicle?*

_____

_____

_____

4. *Prior to sending the lifted prints off to be entered into the automated fingerprint database for comparison, whose fingerprints would you want to take to compare to the ones found on the car?*

_____

_____

5. *Is a fingerprint **direct** or **circumstantial** evidence? Why?*

_____

_____

_____

_____

WHAT IS A LATENT FINGERPRINT?

Latent fingerprints are those fingerprints that are found at a crime scene, which are visible, or invisible. These prints are the result of an oily residue that is produced by the skin. In some cases, the print is visible. This is especially true if the suspect had blood on his or her hands and the fingerprint was made in blood or the fingerprint is embedded in putty or other material such as wet paint. An embedded type of fingerprint is known as a *plastic* print. In other cases, the print has to be developed by using a fine powder of contrasting color from the background of the print. In other words, when lifting a fingerprint from the side of a white refrigerator, the officer would choose black fingerprint dust and a white latent card. Fingerprints are generally found on smooth surfaces such as glass, metal, or wood. The purpose of processing the print is to make it visible. In cases where a print is visible, a photograph is normally taken. If a bloody palm print was found on a wall in a homicide scene, the section of the wall may very well be removed and taken into evidence. Objects that can be moved to a crime lab will be taken from the scene and processed later. If, for example, a jewelry box needed to be processed, the patrol officer working the burglary would pick it up with rubber gloves, place it in a bag and transport it to the lab for processing rather than processing it in the field. At the lab, the jewelry box may be placed into a fish tank with a lid. A few squirts of superglue are placed on a small tin foil dish in the tank. Within twenty-four hours the fumes from the glue react with the oily deposits in the fingerprints and they turn white. These prints are then photographed and can be used for comparison.

There are several different types of chemicals and processes that are used to process latent prints. The most common is the fingerprint dusting method. The powder is made from ground-up volcanic rock and generally comes in black and light gray. A small amount of contrasting powder is lightly brushed over the area where prints are suspected. Once a print is discovered, the officer lightly brushes over the print to remove excess powder and to develop it. It is very important to use this powder sparingly. It tends to get on everything. Many police departments have had property damage and cleaning expenses sent to them by victims after careless officers used too much powder at a scene. After the print is developed, lifting media (tape) is used to remove the print from the object and place it on a latent card.

There are different types of lifting media. The most common is transparent cellulose tape. This tape is similar to scotch tape and comes in different widths. Hinged lifters also come in different sizes and consist of a clear plastic side with a protective cover and a card. To use this, the protective cover is removed which reveals the sticky tape-like surface. The sticky surface is placed on the dusted print and then peeled off. This is then folded over onto the card. It's a combination tape and card apparatus.

There are numerous methods for processing latent prints. Fumes from iodine, silver nitrate, and ninhydren are expelled from pumps, cans, and other devices onto the area where prints are suspected. The chemicals react with the oily residues in the prints and become visible. These types of chemicals should only be used by experts as they can be extremely toxic and hazardous. Iron filings and a magnetic brush can be used in some cases to develop fingerprints. Superglue is a commonly used substance in crime labs as was described earlier. One of the most dramatic developments in processing latent prints came with the invention of the laser or alternative light source. With this portable light and colored lenses, the investigator can recover latent prints that were all but impossible to obtain before. The equipment includes a laser light source, a variety of different-colored powders and colored eyeglasses. The investigator powders the area, and the light source combined with the special glasses makes the latent prints glow. It is somewhat similar to the invisible stamp placed on the back of the hand of a nightclub patron.

Two days after your vehicle was burglarized the investigator assigned to the case called and asked to meet with you. When the investigator came by your house, he asked you who had access to your car. Whose fingerprints could be found on and in your car? You advised that you keep your car very clean and that the only people who had been in the car since you had cleaned it was yourself and your brother. He had you and your brother come down to the station so that your fingerprints could be added to the case file and be eliminated from the unknown latent prints lifted from your car. He advised that this process is accomplished by rolling prints on a "ten card" and having them compared. At the police station, you and your brother are brought into an area designated for taking fingerprints. There is a table with a metal fingerprint cardholder and what looks like a large ink stamp pad next to it. This type of inking device is known as a *porelon pad.* You are told by the technician to relax and let him do all of the work. He takes your hand and individually rolls each finger in the ink and then in the square box on the card. This is known as a *rolled print.* Then he takes your thumbs and makes straight-down prints on the bottom. He takes the remaining four fingers and does the same in the larger boxes provided. These are known as *plain or simultaneous* prints. It is extremely important that the prints are clear and not smudged. While the technician was rolling your brother's prints, the investigator advised you that the next step was to have the fingerprint examiner compare the rolled prints to the latent lifts. This is accomplished by identifying unique points that are identical on both prints. After the examiner has located nine to twelve such points, the prints are determined to be a match.

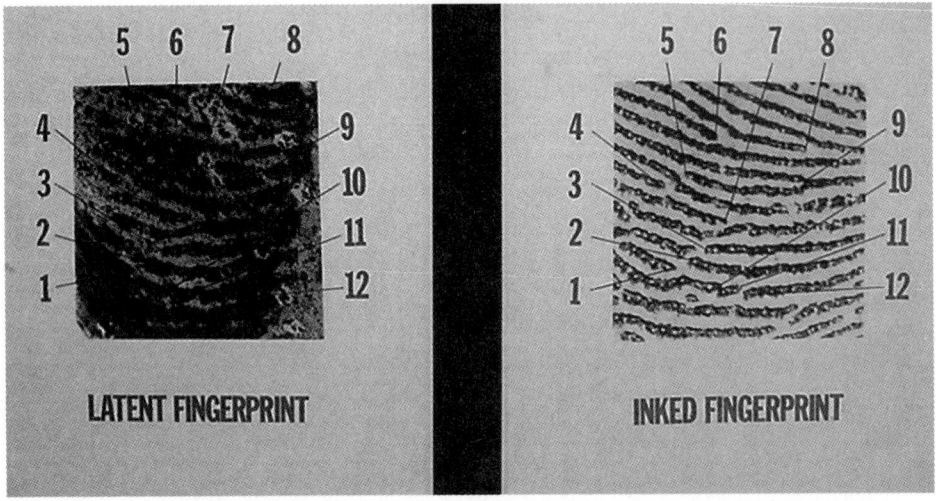

(Courtesy of the Seminole County Sheriff's Office Latent Print Unit)

Every day, people who need their prints taken for employment purposes go to police departments around the country for this service. Employers check the background of potential employees by using fingerprints. Anyone who has been arrested has had their fingerprints taken and those prints are on record. These cards are entered into the database of the *Automated Fingerprint Identification System* (AFIS). Only cards that are clear and readable can be entered; all others are returned to the department.

This system enables local police departments to submit unknown latent prints taken from crime scenes to be compared to the national database. The computer selects several possibilities based upon similar points of identification. A fingerprint examiner then visually checks the prints selected against the latent prints. A certified latent print examiner makes the actual identification, not the computer. The computer only "narrows the field." The purpose of all fingerprint technology is to make identification against existing records. If no record exists to compare the latent prints, than no

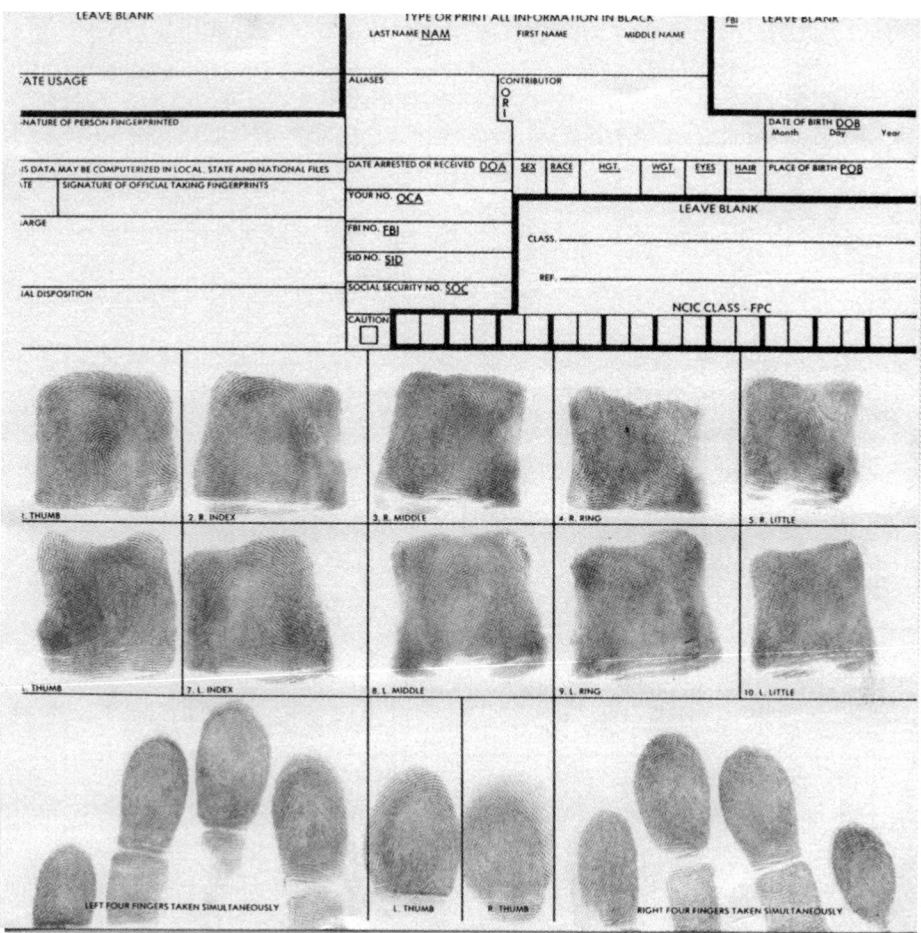

identification can be made. This is especially true of juvenile offenders who have not yet been processed. In Florida, fingerprint cards are sent to the Florida Department of Law Enforcement (FDLE) and the Federal Bureau of Investigation (FBI). The agency that created the printed card also keeps one on record. The types of fingerprint cards that are used most commonly include the *application card,* which is used for employment purposes, the *arrest card* required after every arrest, and the *personal identification card* that is usually done at the request of parents for their children. Arrest cards are either adult or juvenile. The juvenile card is usually a different color and has the word JUVENILE boldly printed on the top. This is to prevent juvenile records from being mistakenly entered into adult records.

1. What are the types of latent prints that are found on a crime scene?

_____

_____

_____

2. What is fingerprint powder used for, and what is it normally made out of?

_____

_____

_____

3. What is the clear plastic tape used for in fingerprinting?

_____

_____

_____

4. What should be written on the latent lift card?

_____

_____

_____

5. Why is it important to obtain clear prints on a ten-card?

_____

_____

_____

_____

A week after you and your brother were at the station, the investigator called to advise that he had a suspect. While the investigator was reviewing the pawnshop report, which lists all of the transactions that take place in pawnshops, he notices one man had pawned five car stereos. He checked the man's criminal background and found that he had been convicted several times for burglary and grand theft. One of the stereos was of the same make and model that you reported stolen. The suspect's ten-card was checked against a thumbprint taken from inside your car, and it was positively identified as his. The investigator recovered the pawn ticket. The thumbprint on the ticket was also compared to his ten-card and matched the suspect. A warrant was issued for the subject for burglary, grand theft, and dealing in stolen property.

About a month after the warrant was issued, the suspect, Harvey Frollik, was arrested outside a rundown motel. The sheriff's warrant squad arrested him. At the jail he was searched, photographed, and fingerprinted. The correction's officer assigned to fingerprint the suspect is skilled at obtaining excellent prints. He placed the card in the cardholder and then put three dabs of printer's ink on a glass slab next to the cardholder. He used a rubber roller to smooth out the ink into a fine, even application. The fingerprint bench is approximately elbow height and normally located against a wall. Because of the large number of suspects processed at the jail, it is cost-effective to use the printers' ink method rather than the more costly porelon pad. The officer directed the suspect to a sink and had him wash and dry his hands thoroughly. The officer then took the suspect's hand and began with his right thumb and then in order, each finger. He inked the finger and then rolled it from nail bed to nail bed and from the fingertip to one-quarter inch below the first joint of the finger onto the card. The thumb was rolled toward the suspect and the fingers away. This technique prevents the suspect from being placed in an awkward and uncomfortable position. Once the ten-card is completed, the suspect and the officer must sign the card. The officer must make sure that the card is completely filled out and that all of the information is correct. While he was rolling the suspect's fingers, the officer noticed that the middle finger of the suspect's left hand was missing the top digit. In the space provided for this print, the officer wrote *amputated*. This is the appropriate notation. If the finger was injured and wrapped, the officer would have written *bandaged*. If the suspect had arthritis and his hands were crippled, the officer would have cut the card into strips, placed the strips in a coroner's spoon, inked the finger, and moved the card around the fingers to obtain the print. Then, he would have reassembled the ten-card and made a notation as to the condition of the suspect's hands. If the subject had excessive perspiration, the officer would dry each finger individually or use alcohol to dry them. If the suspect had smooth fingerprints, which are often found in elderly persons, a ridge builder would have been used. A ridge builder is either a commercial product specifically for this purpose or a small amount of petroleum jelly could be used. If, after rolling the suspects prints, they were still not clear, the officer would have to ensure the fingers are clean, adjust pressure on the card and vary the amount of ink used. In some cases, such as with a concrete worker, the fingerprints are extremely rough and notations must be made on the card to explain. After rolling the prints, the officer cleaned the equipment with denatured alcohol. (Benzine or commercial products could be used as well.) Paper towels are not used in the cleaning of this equipment, as they would leave lint like deposits. After the initial processing, the fingerprint cards are added to the suspect's record and then copies are forwarded to FDLE and the FBI.

Law enforcement and corrections officers are trained to roll fingerprints in their academies. A poor job of obtaining prints speaks loudly as to the individual officer's attention to detail and pride in work. A defective fingerprint card is returned through the chain of command back to the officer with notations as to discrepancies. One of the most common problems is failure to sign the card and missing details on the card. Another reason for return is lack of ridge detail on the prints. The ridges on the fingerprint must show up clearly on the fingerprint card. If they are smudged or if there was not enough ink used, they are unreadable. If the suspect moves and smudges the fingerprint card, than a new card must be started and the smudged one thrown away. If a fingerprint examiner cannot read the fingerprint card, it is worthless.

As a general rule, you only have one opportunity to obtain these prints. This is especially true with latent prints at a crime scene. Even after an arrest, if the suspect bonds out or is released and the ten-card is returned, there is not much likelihood of getting another chance. In some cases, this could have very serious implications. A serial killer normally has several minor arrests prior to becoming a serial killer. An officer not paying attention while doing the ten-card for a petty theft could result in the card not being entered into the Automated Fingerprint Identification System (AFIS). The fact that these prints were not entered into the Automated Fingerprint Identification System could lead to the serial killer not being identified and continuing to kill as a result. The only way to become proficient at lifting latent prints and obtaining legible fingerprint cards is through practice.

FINGERPRINT PATTERS AND CLASSIFICATIONS

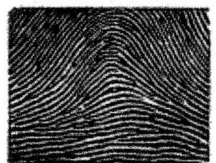 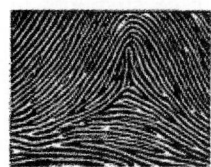  

PLAIN ARCHES

In plain arches the ridges enter on one side of the impression and flow or tend to flow out the other side with a rise or wave in the center.

TENTED ARCHES

Tented arches are similar to plain arches with the exception that the ridges in the center form a definite angle; or one or more ridges at the center form an upthrust; or they approach the loop type, possessing two of the basic characteristics of the loop but lacking in the third.

ULNAR LOOPS

Ulnar loops are those types of patterns in which the loops flow in the direction of the little fingers.

RADIAL LOOPS

Radial loops are those types of patterns in which the loops flow toward the thumbs.

 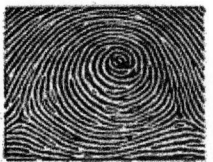  

DOUBLE LOOP

The double loop consists of two separate loop formations, with two separate and distinct sets of shoulders and two deltas.

PLAIN WHORL

A plain whorl has two deltas and at least one ridge making a complete circuit, which may be spiral, oval, or any variant of the circle,. An imaginary line drawn between the two deltas must touch or cross at least one of the recurving ridges within the pattern area.

CENTRAL POCKET WHORL

The central pocket whorl consists of one or more recurving ridges, or an obstruction at right angles to the inner line of flow, with two deltas between which an imaginary line would cut or touch no recurving ridge within the pattern area. The inner line of flow of a central pocket loop is determined by drawing an imaginary line between the inner delta and the center of the innermost recurve or looping ridge.

ACCIDENTAL WHORL

The accidental whorl is a pattern with two or more deltas, and a combination of two or more different types of patterns exclusive of the plain arch. This classification also includes those exceedingly unusual patterns which may not be placed by definition into any other classes.

(http://www.adtdl.army.mil/cgi-bin/atdl.dll/fm/19-20/toc.htm)

Identify your fingerprint patterns and write them in the following spaces:

Left Hand

_____ _____ _____ _____ _____

Right Hand

_____ _____ _____ _____ _____

   thumb   *index*   *middle*   *ring*   *little finger*

SUMMARY

In this chapter, we discussed the relationship of latent fingerprints left at a crime scene and rolled prints on a fingerprint card. We defined what a latent print was and identified the types of fingerprints found at a crime scene and on what type of surfaces they may be found. The purpose for developing the latent print and methods used to develop them was also identified, as was the proper use of contrasting powders in developing the prints. We also discussed when to develop a print in the field and when to use the lab. The various methods of latent lifting media were also identified. The importance of obtaining clear fingerprints on a ten-card was stressed, as was its proper routing. The types of fingerprint cards were identified as was the equipment used in the obtaining these prints. The general procedures used in the fingerprinting of individuals were discussed as were procedures for fingerprinting people with special problems. The criterion used for an acceptable print card was identified as was common reasons for the return of the fingerprint cards.

CROSSWORD PUZZLE

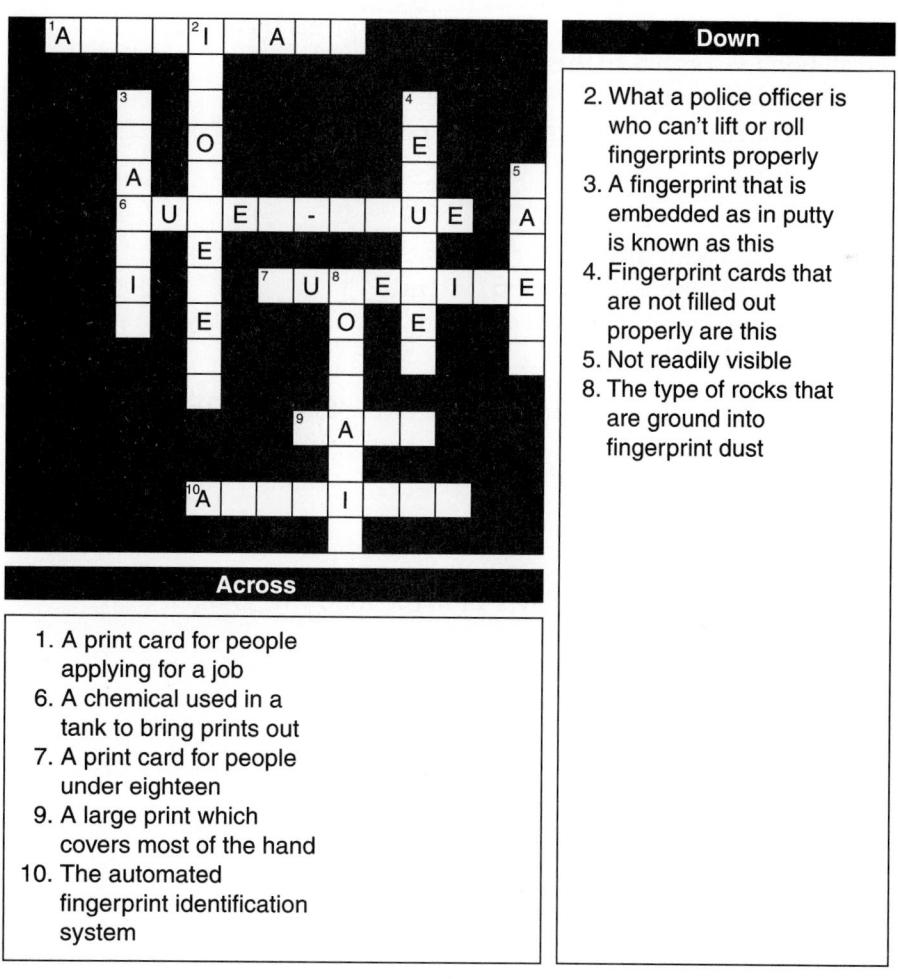

Down

2. What a police officer is who can't lift or roll fingerprints properly
3. A fingerprint that is embedded as in putty is known as this
4. Fingerprint cards that are not filled out properly are this
5. Not readily visible
8. The type of rocks that are ground into fingerprint dust

Across

1. A print card for people applying for a job
6. A chemical used in a tank to bring prints out
7. A print card for people under eighteen
9. A large print which covers most of the hand
10. The automated fingerprint identification system

Test Your Knowledge

For each multiple choice question select the *best* possible answer.

1. Any fingerprints, visible or not, that may be found on a crime scene are known as:
   a. plastic.
   b. visible.
   c. latent.
   d. none of the above.

2. The purpose of developing latent fingerprints is to:
   a. make them visible and collectible for possible identification.
   b. use them as evidence in court.
   c. place them on fingerprint cards.
   d. catch the bad guy.

3. The methods used to develop latent prints include all of the following except:
   a. powders.
   b. iodine.
   c. carpenter's glue.
   d. ninhydrin.

4. A guideline to follow when powdering and lifting prints includes:
   a. bring all portable objects to the lab for processing.
   b. do not powder a print unless it is necessary.
   c. do not lift a latent impression unless it is necessary.
   d. all of the above.

5. *AFIS* stands for:
   a. automated fingerprint investigator station.
   b. automated fingerprint identification system.
   c. automatic fingerprint impression standard.
   d. none of the above.

6. The routing of a fingerprint card includes all of the following except:
   a. the arresting officer.
   b. the originating agency.
   c. the state police.
   d. the FBI.

7. The standard fingerprint card includes all of the following except:
   a. applicant.
   b. criminal.
   c. non-criminal.
   d. juvenile.

8. Fingerprints should be taken in this order:
   a. roll the thumb toward the subject's body.
   b. roll the fingers away from the subject's body.
   c. roll the thumb away from the subject's body.
   d. a and b.

9. If a suspect has crippled hands:
    a. the fingers must be forced into position.
    b. a coroner's spoon could be used.
    c. the card can be cut in strips and moved around the finger.
    d. b and c.

10. Reasons for returning fingerprint cards include:
    a. lack of sufficient ridge detail.
    b. lack of complete identifying information.
    c. lack of signatures.
    d. all of the above.

6

Evidence Handling Procedures and Chain of Custody Concepts

The concept of evidence is one of the basic foundations of all legal systems. Evidence questions are argued in every courtroom in the country. In some cultures, evidence of criminal acts are demonstrated by placing a red-hot knife on the tongue of an accused criminal. If it sticks, the accused is guilty; if not the person is innocent. This type of evidence is not allowed in our system of law. Although trial by ordeal has been used historically in many cultures, its validity is questionable at best. The basis could be that a guilty person might have a dryer mouth than an innocent person and the resulting red-hot knife sticking to the person's tongue would indicate a degree of nervousness found in a guilty mind. This may be found in the guilty man confessing rather than going through the ordeal. It is difficult at best to determine where this type of proof got its start.

WHAT IS *EVIDENCE?*

Evidence is *anything* that logically proves or disproves a fact at issue. Whether you are aware of it or not, you use evidence daily. Did you ever go to the refrigerator and grab the milk container only to find a quarter of an inch in the bottom? Who did it? How did you determine this *fact?* You conducted an investigation, and in doing so, you gathered evidence. It might have been testimonial evidence from a younger sister, who acted as an informant. It might have come from witnessing your brother drinking a glass of milk, shortly before or after you discovered the offense. Both of these are kinds of evidence.

When you think of evidence, you normally think of courtrooms and trials. Evidence is all around us. Especially *trace evidence.* Trace evidence is comprised of anything that is left at the scene of a crime, which leads the investigator to the suspect. In the case of your brother, you would have found his fingerprints all over the milk container. That might place him at the scene but does not indicate that he was the culprit. Remember that fingerprints are only meaningful if the suspect had no business where they were found. Your brother is in the refrigerator all the time and had taken milk out of this container prior to the offensive quarter-inch left in the bottom crime. If he had spilt the milk on the floor, there might have been footwear impressions in front of the refrigerator. If he was wearing a sweater, fibers from this garment might have been left inside the refrigerator or on the milk container itself. If he wrote a note to your mother to buy some more milk, this would have been documentary evidence implicating him in the crime. Had he dropped his glass of milk on the floor and it broke, traces of the glass could be recovered from the area and be used as evidence. Although these examples are somewhat ridiculous, the types of evidence presented are very real. When a case is serious enough to warrant summoning a forensic team, all of these types of minute evidence are extremely important and collected.

Ballistic evidence can demonstrate whether a particular weapon fired a projectile used in the homicide. Ballistics is the study of firearms and the projectiles that are fired from them. Ballistic evidence includes matching a bullet from a specific firearm. This is done by comparing the markings on the bullet with the rifling inside the barrel of the gun. This is very similar to a fingerprint in its uniqueness. Actual fingerprints can be found on firearm casings located at the scene of a shooting. DNA can be obtained from blood, hairs, and seminal fluid and used to positively identify a suspect. In cases where vehicles have hit and run, paint transfer and glass fragments can be used to identify the vehicle. During every autopsy, a toxicology report is generated to determine the presence of drugs in the body of the victim. This can be valuable in determining cause of death. In every burglary investigation, it is important to locate the point of entry. This can be accomplished by locating pry or tool marks around the door or window that was used to enter the scene.

SCENARIO NUMBER ONE:
Evidence

It's Saturday morning at 2:45 A.M. You are summoned to an apparent homicide scene at 1200 Oak Avenue. Upon your arrival, the patrol officer who responded to a disturbance and discovered the body briefed you. The crime scene technicians are already there and photographing the scene. The first responding officer advised that he responded to a disturbance that involved a loud argument and glass breaking. When he arrived there was no noise and the front door was open. Inside was the victim who had been stabbed to death possibly by a broken bottle. On the floor next to the body was a broken whiskey bottle with a great deal of blood on it. The neighbor advised that another man was drinking with the victim, and later they both got drunk and loud. After a while, they began to fight and that is when the neighbor called the police. The witness advised that the argument was over money that was owed to the victim, and she heard distinctively something about an IOU. On the coffee table there was a blood-spattered piece of paper with IOU written on it.

1. Identify the different kinds of evidence present at this scene:

_____

_____

_____

_____

2. What can be proved or disproved by this evidence?

_____

_____

_____

3. What kind of evidence does the witness provide, and how can the investigator use this evidence?

_____

_____

_____

_____

4. What is the responsibility of the first responding officer in this case?

_____

_____

_____

_____

5. What is the first thing that the crime scene technicians should do before anything else?

_____

_____

_____

_____

6. What is the main function of the investigator in this case?

_____

_____

_____

_____

When an officer collects evidence, he or she marks the evidence and places it into a bag or container. The container is sealed with evidence tape, and the initials of the recovering officer are affixed to the tape and the bag. The date, time, location, and case number are filled in on the form, which is usually attached to the bag or container. On that form, the officer acknowledges that he or she is the recovering officer. When the officer turns in the evidence, the evidence custodian will sign the document indicating receipt of the evidence. Any time the evidence is handled or processed, the name and identity of the individual is logged on the chain of custody document as well as the reason for handling or processing. The witnessed, written record of all individuals who have maintained unbroken control over the evidence since its acquisition is known as the *chain of custody*. The chain of custody will identify who had the evidence, when, why, and what changes if any were made to the evidence. It proves that the evidence that was collected at the scene is the same evidence that is presented in court.

SCENARIO NUMBER TWO:

The Residential Burglary

You are dispatched to 704 Elm Street in reference to a burglary. At the scene, you discover that the point of entry was the kitchen window. On the ground below the window is a yellow-handled flat-ended screwdriver. The screwdriver has a corner of the tip missing. Your case number is 00-124-9882. You will turn in the evidence to Sgt. Mike Jones. You are employed by the Nelsonville Police Department. On the following page, fill out the evidence bag label and then complete the request for analysis form which follows.

SCENARIO NUMBER THREE:

The Overdose

It is late Wednesday afternoon; you are scheduled to go on vacation tomorrow. You are summoned to a crime scene involving a drug overdose. Upon your arrival at the scene, Officer Frolic is walking around the crime scene with two containers of white powder. No one is posted at the front door and the scene is not secured. The crime scene technicians have not arrived, and nothing has been processed. Officer Frolic advises that the deceased's girlfriend picked up the containers off of the dresser and gave them to him. Officer Frolic stated that he would put them *right where they were found* so that you could collect them for evidence. You advise him that he will have to submit the evidence sheet, chain of custody, and the evidence to the evidence custodian. You asked him if he processed the containers for prints, and he became angry and walked away with the evidence. You then asked him for the information and location of the girlfriend. He advised that he didn't catch her name and that he let her go because she had to go to work. Fearful at the state of contamination and lack of protection on this scene, you contact the lieutenant and advise her of the situation. Your lieutenant contacts the patrol lieutenant and another officer is sent for security. The crime scene technicians arrive and begin to process the scene. You interview the family and friends of the deceased and determine that it was a probable overdose. At the station you contact the evidence custodian and request to view the evidence. The evidence custodian brings out two bags that Officer Frolic submitted. One bag had a quantity of white powder and the other had two containers. There was a request to process the containers for fingerprints and a lab request for analysis of the white substance. Officer Frolic had apparently combined the contents of the two containers (no notation was made on the chain of custody form as to the combination of the two containers).

DEPARTMENT: _____   CASE NUMBER: _____

EVIDENCE

DESCRIPTION:
_____
_____

REMOVED FROM:
_____
_____

ADDRESS:
_____
_____

TIME:_____   DATE: _____

SECURED BY:
_____
_____

RELEASED TO: _____
LOCATION: _____
TIME:_____ DATE: _____ SIGNATURE: _____

RELEASED TO: _____
LOCATION: _____
TIME:_____ DATE: _____ SIGNATURE: _____

RELEASED TO: _____
LOCATION: _____
TIME:_____ DATE: _____ SIGNATURE: _____

NOTES:
_____
_____

1. Identify the errors made by Officer Frolic:

_____
_____
_____
_____

DEPARTMENT: _____   CASE NUMBER: _____

CRIME LABORATORY REQUEST FOR PROCESSING OR ANALYSIS

OFFICER:_____   ID: _____

DEPARTMENT PHONE NUMBER: _____

TYPE OF CASE:_____

DATE:_____   VICTIM: _____

DESCRIPTION:
_____
_____

REMOVED FROM:
_____
_____

ADDRESS:
_____
_____

TYPE OF PROCESSING OR ANALYSIS REQUESTED:
_____
_____
_____

FINDINGS:
_____
_____
_____
_____

BY: _____   DATE: _____
    LABORATORY TECHNICIAN

2. *What types of legal problems could occur with the admissibility of the evidence in Officer Frolic's case? Why?*

_____

_____

_____

_____

3. How does the girlfriend at the scene fit into this case? What needs to be done?

_____

_____

_____

4. What type of crime has been committed if any? Why?

_____

_____

_____

Officer Frolic was brought before Internal Affairs and was disciplined for his actions. He received a letter of reprimand and was ordered to attend refresher courses on basic crime scene procedures at the academy. The crime lab received the bag with the substances. At the lab, a technician signed the chain of custody and took possession of the evidence. Prior to processing the substance, the crime lab technician made an incision on the bag, removed a sample of the substance and then sealed the bag with evidence tape. His initials and date were written across the tape. When the substance was analyzed, it was determined that there were two types of substances: cocaine and heroin. The autopsy results also confirmed the presence of both these substances in the body of the deceased. When someone dies as the result of ingesting substances such as these, it is not unusual to charge the person who supplied the individual with the substances that killed him or her with murder. The girlfriend was located and interviewed. She advised that they were both using the substances when he died. In an effort to cooperate and reduce the likelihood of a prison sentence, she gave the police the names and addresses of the drug dealers that supplied the drugs. After making several controlled purchases of heroin and cocaine under the supervision of drug agents, the drug dealers were charged with numerous major controlled substance violations and homicide.

Evidence must be handled very carefully. There is no room for sloppy work or a careless attitude. The chain of custody must be maintained. The evidence must be kept free from contamination. When evidence is submitted, a sufficient quantity must be available to be analyzed. In some cases, only a minute piece of cocaine is recovered in a drug case. Once it is analyzed there is nothing left to use as evidence. It was lost in the process. When evidence is submitted for analysis, there must be a standard to compare against. In the event of a sexual battery, pubic hair from the victim is always taken to compare against unknown pubic hair found on the scene. If it doesn't belong to the victim, then it is quite possibly the suspect's. Once a suspect is developed, then pubic hair is removed from him for comparison.

One of the first duties of an officer in relation to evidence is to *determine and identify the evidence.* Walking up to a robbery scene you may very well step over an old rusty screwdriver lying on the ground next to the curb. Once inside, the clerk advises that a man robbed her with a screwdriver. Determining what is evidence is not as easy as you may think. *Anything* can be evidence. Prior to processing any evidence, it must be photographed. The screwdriver may be there by coincidence, or it may be the weapon used in the crime. The officer collecting it must be careful not to get his or her prints on it. Rubber gloves would be advisable and only handle the screwdriver at the point. Even with rubber gloves, prints can be damaged from handling. Once placed in the plastic bag, the officer seals it with evidence tape and initials and dates it over the seal. The form on the bag must be completed and signed prior to submission along with a request for tech services to process the screwdriver for prints.

It is the officer's responsibility to preserve the evidence. In a scene with a great deal of evidence to be recovered, the officer must determine what should be collected first. Fragile evidence is always collected first. Once evidence is collected, it must be marked or tagged. This depends upon the type of evidence. A handgun could be tagged or inscribed with a case number. In cases where evidence was held for trial, the evidence is returned after the trial to the owner. This is done once there is no further need for the evidence to be held. In some cases, the evidence is returned to the owner prior to the trial. This is done when there is no question as to the ownership. In shoplifting cases, the store retains the evidence for trial and it does not get placed into evidence.

Different types of evidence require various methods of collection. A blood-soaked garment would not be placed in a plastic bag. If it were, it would decompose into something unrecognizable. A revolver could be placed in a clear evidence bag unloaded. Narcotics are normally placed into clear plastic bags, as are documents. All bagged evidence is prepared basically the same. Evidence tape is used to seal the bag and the initials of the recovering officer along with the date are written across the tape. The chain of custody form is completed and adhered to the front of the bag, and if analysis is requested, a separate form is executed for that purpose. Hair, fiber, and paint chips are minute evidence that are best placed into small envelopes. Glass and flammables are best placed in metal cans. The glass can cut through most bags, and flammable evidence from arson such as ashes with traces of gasoline are best secured in metal, as they can be a fire hazard. Seminal fluid is most commonly found on clothing or bedding. This type of evidence is best turned in for analysis after air-drying and storage in paper bags. Blood evidence can be taken in the same manner.

Evidence must be stored properly. In a movie about police corruption, a large magnet was placed next to the videotape of a crime. The magnet wiped out the evidence. In this case, it was intentional. Regardless of this, the evidence was not protected. The evidence room must be secure. Only authorized personnel must have access. If the security of this area is breached, all of the evidence stored there becomes questionable. The question of who has access to the storage area is regularly asked in court. The collection, storage, and analysis of evidence is crucial to our criminal justice system. If the evidence is obtained illegally, it cannot be used even if it was not intentionally done. In addition, anything that is discovered as the result of the illegally obtained evidence being processed will not be allowed in court. This is known as the *exclusionary rule* and falls under the fruit of the poisonous tree doctrine. The fruit of the poisonous tree is a phrase that describes tainted evidence. Once evidence has been discovered in an illegal manner, any evidence found as the result cannot be used. The evidence that is tainted or illegally obtained "poisons" the whole tree (of evidence), and no evidence can be used that has grown from it. If a problem exists with the evidence that an officer has collected, he or she must advise the prosecutor immediately as this could seriously change the trial strategy and jeopardize the case. As the result of the exclusionary rule, the guilty go free. This may sound like a bad thing, but in reality, it protects all of our rights against unlawful government intrusion. Evidence must also have scientific value. It must be able to show or demonstrate relationships such as a fingerprint and the fingers of the suspect. Occasionally a movie will have a psychic reader being used to help the police; this is a rare occurrence and is generally used only as a last resort. Evidence is used to prove or disprove a fact at issue in a court of law. If reasonable doubt is established by the defense as to the reliability of the evidence or of its value as evidence, credibility is lost and so is the evidence.

Proof is the result of evidence.

SUMMARY

In this chapter, we discussed the importance of evidence collection. We defined relevant evidence and identified trace evidence. We discussed the different types of evidence found at crime scenes, and the areas that impact the admissibility of evidence. The chain of custody was defined and explained in detail, as was the importance of maintaining the chain of custody in a criminal case. We completed an evidence label and a request for analysis form. Standards of evidence, protection of evidence from contamination, and submission standards were also identified. We also reviewed the responsibilities of the officer in relation to evidence, as were methods of collection, preserving, marking, and transporting various types of evidence.

CROSSWORD PUZZLE

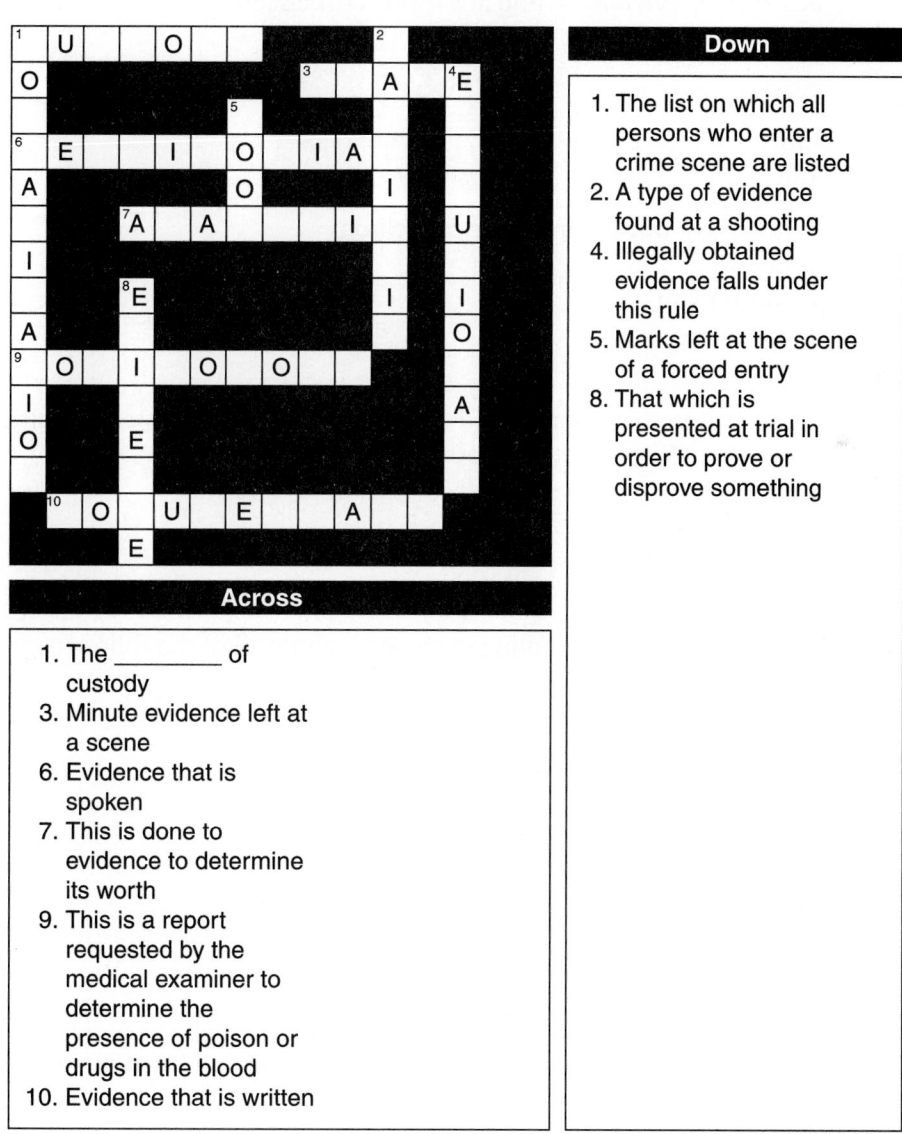

Down

1. The list on which all persons who enter a crime scene are listed
2. A type of evidence found at a shooting
4. Illegally obtained evidence falls under this rule
5. Marks left at the scene of a forced entry
8. That which is presented at trial in order to prove or disprove something

Across

1. The _____ of custody
3. Minute evidence left at a scene
6. Evidence that is spoken
7. This is done to evidence to determine its worth
9. This is a report requested by the medical examiner to determine the presence of poison or drugs in the blood
10. Evidence that is written

Test Your Knowledge

For each multiple choice question select the best possible answer.

1. Anything that logically tends to prove or disprove a material fact at issue is known as:
   a. circumstantial evidence.
   b. reliable evidence.
   c. trace evidence.
   d. relevant evidence.

2. Minute articles that assist an investigator in locating a suspect are known as:
   a. circumstantial evidence.
   b. reliable evidence.
   c. trace evidence.
   d. relevant evidence.

3. Common types of trace evidence found at various crime scenes include all of the following except:
   a. blood.
   b. hair.
   c. photo album.
   d. seminal fluid.

4. Areas that have the most impact on evidence include:
   a. legal requirements.
   b. emotional requirements.
   c. scientific value.
   d. a and c.

5. The _____ is the witnessed, written record of all individuals who have maintained unbroken control over the evidence since its acquisition.
   a. circle of truth
   b. rope of record
   c. chain of custody
   d. string of events

6. Important considerations when handling evidence include all of the following except:
   a. submit sufficient quantities of evidence.
   b. maintain chain of custody.
   c. submit unknown standards of evidence.
   d. protect evidence from contamination.

7. It is important to advise the prosecutor of:
   a. the trial date.
   b. any potential problems with the evidence.
   c. who the best judge is.
   d. what day is good for you to have a trial.

8. The chain of custody establishes:
   a. proof that the evidence collected is the same that is being presented in court.
   b. ownership.
   c. relative believability.
   d. none of the above.

9. Evidence must be:
   a. properly collected.
   b. properly marked.
   c. properly protected.
   d. all of the above.

10. Proof is:
   a. the result of a good prosecutor.
   b. in the pudding.
   c. the result of evidence.
   d. up to the jury.

CHAPTER 7

Crimes Against Property Preliminary Investigation Protection of Archaeological Sites and Artifacts

How does a crime against property differ from other types of crimes? Property crimes are non-violent and do not involve force, threats of force, or the placing of victims in fear in order to obtain their valuables.

SCENARIO NUMBER ONE:

The Department Store

A man enters a department store. He proceeds to the shoe department and looks at several pairs of shoes. He checks the area to see if anyone is observing him, and then he tries on a pair of new shoes. He places his old shoes in the box and exits the store wearing the new shoes. Right before he exits the store, he pauses and looks around. He observes a man looking directly at him, gesturing at him to return to the shoe department. At this point, the thief bolts through the door and runs into the parking lot with the security officer giving pursuit. The police observe a man fitting the description of the shoplifter and detain him three blocks from the store. The store security officer is transported to where the suspect is detained and identifies him as the thief and the shoes on his feet as the same ones that were stolen from the store. This procedure is known as a *show-up* and is used to identify a suspect. Show-ups are only used if a short period of time has elapsed and only if the victim can identify the suspect. The shoes are valued at ninety-nine dollars. This is a misdemeanor that did not take place in your presence.

You are the police officer assigned to this call.

Can you arrest the suspect based upon the above scenario? If so, what is your probable cause? If not, why?

_____

_____

_____

_____

What is (are) the crime(s) that took place?

_____

_____

_____

What is the difference between a show-up and a line-up?

_____

_____

_____

The most common type of property crime is theft. As in the example above, shoplifting is a very common crime and costs businesses millions of dollars in losses a year. Internal theft combined with shoplifting is termed "shrinkage" by the industry. Shrinkage refers to the loss of profit. These losses are passed on to the consumer. Internal theft can take several different forms. A cash register operator could bypass the scanning device and charge a family member $25.00 for groceries which actually total $125.00. In many stores, cameras are used to watch for shoplifters *and* employees who may be stealing. In cases of theft, an officer must determine when the stolen object was last seen, what the object was, how it can be identified, who the legal owner is, who discovered the theft, if any witnesses were present, and if the item(s) were insured.

SCENARIO NUMBER TWO:
The Potato Chips

A potato chip delivery person left his truck unsecured and returned to find that several cases of chips were taken from the truck while he or she was in the store. The potato chip route person called to report that three cases of potato chips were stolen off her truck, and you are the responding officer to the scene.

What questions would you ask the victim as a part of your investigation?

_____

_____

_____

_____

_____

_____

What crime(s) has (have) been committed?

_____

_____

While you are taking the report, an elderly witness advised that he observed two kids running with the boxes of chips, and they went into the woods behind the store.

What do you do now?

_____

_____

In the woods you find an eighteen-year-old and a sixteen-year-old with the chips.

What do you do now?

_____

_____

How can you prove that they did it?

_____

_____

The potato chip route person was a victim of a vehicle burglary and theft. The vehicle burglary is a felony and the potato chip theft is a misdemeanor. A back-up officer should have brought the witness to the location of the two suspects. This is provided that the officer didn't leave the scene in a rush to capture the chip thieves. If the officer did leave the scene, it would be unlikely that the witness would remain to identify the suspects. If the officer failed to record the information on the witness then later contact for court purposes would be unlikely as well. Without the testimony of the witness, this case would be hard to win in court. The suspects could state that they were walking in the woods and found the chips. If the two suspects were identified as the perpetrators, they would both be arrested for the two crimes mentioned earlier. The adult would be taken to jail, and the juvenile would be taken to juvenile detention.

SCENARIO NUMBER THREE:
The Stolen Car

It is Saturday afternoon, you respond to the shopping mall in reference to a report of a stolen car. The victim is an elderly woman who is extremely upset.

What questions do you ask her?

_____

_____

_____

After placing her in your vehicle and driving around the mall, you find her vehicle parked in the same general location outside a different mall exit. It is not uncommon for people (regardless of age) to forget where they parked.

Name three special considerations you should have when dealing with people who are elderly:

    1. _____

    2. _____

    3. _____

Anytime that you encounter elderly citizens, you should be concerned for their health. The stress of being victimized could bring on or aggravate a medical condition. The fear that they may become confused is very real to them. You should reassure them that it is common for people to become confused and that it happens all of the time. You should also understand that as people reach the age of seventy and eighty, they dread losing their independence. Remember what it felt like when you got your driver's license and could drive solo? Remember your first car? So do they! When they can no longer drive, they have to depend on others, and this is very hard on people who are used to being independent.

SCENARIO NUMBER FOUR:
The Stolen Car

After you left the mall, you were called to the house of a man who is reporting that his vehicle was stolen. As you were asking your first questions in reference to the car, the man's son drove up in the "stolen" car. His son had gotten back from a trip early, and the father didn't know he had taken the car. Many times, family members are not aware of each other's comings and goings. Always ask about the possibility of a family member having the stolen vehicle or any object for that matter. Police spend a great deal of time clearing up cases involving *borrowed* items.

SCENARIO NUMBER FIVE:
The Stolen Truck

After clearing up the confusion in the above case, you are dispatched to a restaurant in reference to a stolen truck. Upon your arrival, you encounter an agitated young man who is demanding that the police do something. You calm him down and ask him to tell you what happened. He relates that he went in to get something to eat and when he came out, his truck was gone.

What question should come to your mind in this case?

_____

_____

When you call the station to ask if there have been any repossession agents active in the area, you are advised that there is one working and that he just picked up a truck. Any time that a person has a vehicle taken in circumstances like the one above, it is important to inquire into his or her payment situation. Is the vehicle paid for? When is the last time the person made a payment? These two questions have cleared up many reported *thefts*.

SCENARIO NUMBER SIX:
The Missing Car

On your way out of the restaurant parking lot, you receive another call in reference to a stolen vehicle. The vehicle owner is at the station and is demanding that something be done. Upon your arrival, the woman demands that you arrest her estranged husband for taking her car.

What do you ask her first?

_____

_____

What can be done for this victim?

_____

_____

_____

Divorce is ugly business. Officers are constantly responding to couples who once cared for one another and now hate with equal passion. If the couple is still married and no property settlement or judgment or other court order has been made by a judge, then the husband can take his wife's car because they are still married. This comes under civil law, and no crime has occurred. It is always important to inquire as to the method in which he took the car. If violence took place, charges of domestic violence may be warranted.

These examples all involve non-crimes. In the event of an actual stolen vehicle, a report must be made including make, model, license plate number, vehicle identification number, and any identifying marks or unique things about the vehicle. A vehicle was recently stolen that had a customized tag. The police tracked the vehicle and apprehended the suspect largely because of the tag. All motor vehicles have vehicle identification numbers. Some of the numbers are easily seen on the dashboard. Others are located on the engine, and some are hidden on the vehicle to assist in the recovery of cars that have been *stripped.* Auto theft investigators use a formula for determining if a VIN has been changed or altered. Not unlike a driver's license, two of the numbers refer to the date that the vehicle was manufactured. If a VIN issued in 1965, was found on 1995 vehicle, the investigator could suppose that the car may have been stolen or assembled from stolen parts. Car thieves sometimes obtain wrecked vehicles and change the VIN onto vehicles that they stole of the same make and model. In cases such as these, investigators will locate the hidden numbers on the vehicle and confirm the finding.

You Are the Patrol Officer

You are on routine patrol. It is Wednesday afternoon. You observe a white four-door passenger car ahead of you. The tag is attached with a coat hanger and appears to be extremely dirty except for fingerprints that stand out. The vehicle is new and clean. As you ride up beside the vehicle, you notice that the rear passenger window has been broken out and the driver keeps looking over and then nervously looking straight ahead. On the driver's door, you notice that the lock has been scratched and is dented. It appears that something is jammed into the mechanism. As you pull behind the vehicle, the passengers keep turning around and looking at you and then saying something to the driver.

What do you do? Why?

_____

_____

_____

Name five indicators of a stolen car:

    1. _____

    2. _____

    3. _____

    4. _____

    5. _____

Every time a police officer approaches a vehicle, special notice must be made of the steering column. If it is broken and the key lock is missing, the car has been possibly stolen. On some occasions, a screwdriver will be found sticking out of the key lock.

When a police officer suspects that a vehicle is stolen, he or she will call in the tag. The dispatcher will take this information and make an inquiry to the National Crime Information Center (NCIC) and the state equivalent. The NCIC database is comprised of all participating states. All reported stolen vehicles and tags are entered into these systems. If the dispatcher determines that the tag is reported stolen, this does not automatically mean that the vehicle is stolen. On rare occasions, duplicate tags are issued by the state. In some cases, a thief switches tags from a similar vehicle that he has stolen and the owner is unaware. Once a vehicle is recovered, it must be removed as stolen from the database. If it is not, than the victim could be stopped for his own stolen vehicle. When a victim is victimized again by the police it is a no-win situation. Officers must always exercise caution and discretion when a tag is reported as stolen. Auto theft investigators use a number of information sources in their investigations. Used car dealers, body shops, insurance companies, the National Automobile Theft Bureau, NCIC, informants, and gas station and parking lot employees are all potential sources of information on stolen vehicles.

SCENARIO NUMBER SEVEN:

The Stolen Tag

It's Monday afternoon; you are on routine patrol. A late-model van runs a stop sign, and you pull it over. While you approach the vehicle, the dispatcher advises that the tag is reported stolen.

What do you do when the driver:

1. Reaches towards the glove compartment or wants to retrieve something from the trunk?

_____

_____

_____

2. Asks to go into his apartment, which is across the street, to get the documents to prove ownership?

_____

_____

_____

3. Asks if he can go use the bathroom at the gas station across the street?

_____

_____

_____

4. Asks to drive to the garage or the police station where you can get out of the weather (it's raining) and "straighten this out"?

_____

_____

5. Has an explanation that gives you reason to doubt the complainants story?

_____

_____

6. Sits in the driver's seat while you check the VIN?

_____

_____

Police officers must always be on guard when it comes to their safety. One of the number one killers of officers is complacency. After being on the job for a number of years and stopping countless people without incident, officers tend to forget the possible danger and take careless risks with their safety. Standing in front of a possible stolen vehicle with the suspect behind the wheel sounds like something that just wouldn't be done. Officers get hurt and worse for being careless. A badge will not stop a moving vehicle. Criminals are extremely good at manipulation. An officer who is duped into believing what a suspect has to say is making a big mistake. If the vehicle has been reported stolen, then it has most probably been stolen regardless of what the driver is reporting. Allowing a suspect to go to the bathroom or into a residence is going to result in the suspect escaping and leaving the suspect in control of the vehicle could result in tragedy.

SCENARIO NUMBER EIGHT:
The Robbery

You just finished roll call in the morning and have finished checking your vehicle. You are dispatched to a residence on Elm Avenue. The complainant advises that he has been "robbed." Upon arrival, you determine that an unknown person entered the residence through the kitchen window during the night and removed a television and surround sound system valued at three thousand dollars. The victim advised that he slept through the night and woke up to discover the incident.

What two crimes have been reported to you?

1. _____

2. _____

The crime of *burglary* is one that does not involve confrontation or violence. A burglary is committed when a person unlawfully enters a structure, residence, or conveyance with the purpose of committing a crime. A person who hides in a business or store while it closes and then breaks out has also committed a burglary. It is committed by stealth and is usually discovered after the burglar has gone. Burglary is a serious felony. The difference between trespass and burglary is the criminal intent of the burglar to commit a crime once inside. *Trespass* is a less serious crime and involves a person unlawfully entering another's property without permission. A trespasser is usually someone who is looking for a place to sleep and has no intent to commit any further crime. The object of the burglar is the value of the property that he or she is going to steal. In the case above, the surround sound and television theft constitute grand theft. The police rarely catch professional burglars. Their crimes are well-prepared and -planned. Police constantly catch juvenile and amateur burglars, as they are generally not prepared and commit crimes without thinking them through. Another type of burglar is the drug addict. Their motivation is to continue to feed their habit. A recovering drug addict remarked that when he went into recovery from his heroin addiction, they had to lay off five cops in Tampa, Florida. He was exaggerating but not by as much as you might think. When a drug-addicted burglar was arrested for two burglaries, he was asked how many he actually did prior to being arrested and his answer was 127 burglaries. He had no reason to lie, as there was no proof in any of the other cases against him. One unusual type of burglar is a *sexual gratification burglar.* He gets sexually excited by the act of entering people's homes and usually takes personal items such as women's underwear. The most common types of burglaries occur in homes and apartments, businesses, conveyances, and other structures such as barns and storage facilities.

Name the five types of burglars:

1. _____

2. _____

3. _____

4. _____

5. _____

One of the most common methods of entry by a burglar involves unlocked or open windows and doors. Today people continue to leave their residences unsecured. Burglars watch television and are aware of products such as the plastic rock that hides the door key. They are also quite familiar with all of the common places for hiding keys. French doors are attractive but are easily opened by breaking out one of the glass panels, and reaching in to unlock the door. Glass doors in general are only secure if double cylinder dead bolt locks with removable keys are used. Once the key is removed, the locked door must be completely smashed out to gain entry. This would cause quite a racket that most burglars would avoid. If the door has its hinges on the outside, the pins may be extracted with a hammer and chisel and the door removed. In the absence of a dead bolt, a credit card or knife could be slipped in between the door's locking mechanism and defeat it. Picking a lock is a method that is not seen often and is most probably used by professional burglars. When there is no sign of forced entry, either the door was left unsecured or the lock was picked. Doors are pried open, doorframes are spread apart with jacks and locks are pulled out of doors by burglars. Sliding glass doors are very common points of entry by burglars. A simple screwdriver can defeat most of these.

Name the four types of burglaries:

1. _____

2. _____

3. _____

4. _____

SCENARIO NUMBER NINE:

The Burglary

You are called to the scene of a burglary. Upon your arrival, the victim advises that he had locked his house prior to leaving for work this morning and when he returned, the front door was open and all of his valuables are missing. You observe the screened porch around the pool in the backyard. The screen doorframe has been spread and the door swings freely back and forth. The sliding glass doors to the house have been taken off their tracks and are leaning against the wall. After searching the house and determining that the perpetrators are gone, you take the victim's statement and then walk through the residence with the victim. The victim will be able to prepare a list of items, which are obviously missing, and will have to follow up later on as more items are discovered to be missing. It is important for the victim to be specific in identifying the missing items by marks or identifying numbers as this will aid in recovery. You observe several areas that have been disturbed and have possible fingerprint evidence. The sergeant arrives and orders crime scene technicians to respond to the residence. You are now free to canvas the neighborhood.

A canvass involves questioning the neighbors about any unusual sounds, movements, or people in the area or leaving the area that can help fix the time of the burglary. The neighbor across the street observed a delivery truck in the driveway and gave a detailed description of two men and the truck. She did not get a tag number but advised that the right-front headlight was out and ACME was printed in large red letters on the side. You remember that at roll call it was mentioned that the investigators were working several burglaries involving trucks. You call the property crime investigators and give them the name of the witness who can possibly identify suspects in this crime and maybe others. Prior to leaving, you discuss with the victim possible improvements he can make to prevent this type of crime from reoccurring. You give him a case number and advise him of the procedures that the department has along with a phone number to call and how to report additional items which he discovers missing.

Name three types of information that you can obtain through a neighborhood canvass:

1. _____

2. _____

3. _____

SCENARIO NUMBER TEN:

The Con

It's Thursday evening. You are dispatched to 134 Pine Street in reference to an unknown problem. Upon your arrival, an elderly man who is extremely upset greets you. You observe a large pile of shingles next to his house and fresh tarpaper on the roof. After you calm him down, you determine that the complaint is based upon a home repair and is possibly a civil issue. You review the basis of the complaint and decide that there is possibly a con game being perpetrated upon the elderly man. A group of roofers approached the man and offered to put a new roof on his house. They set up and began to work by removing all of his shingles. After all of the shingle material was removed, the foreman of the crew asked the owner for cash to buy materials so that they could finish the job. The elderly man gave the foreman four thousand dollars. The crew never returned. There was no contract, and the roofer provided no bond or license to perform the work. The victim advised that the perpetrator's truck had a North Carolina license plate. Every year a group of people who operate home repair fraud schemes travel around the country duping elderly people out of their hard-earned money.

Another con game that is committed using older victims is the *bank examiner swindle*. A man posing as a police officer, investigator, or bank examiner presents identification (usually a badge) to an elderly bank customer. He advises that he is working a case and needs her assistance. The con man convinces the victim to withdraw a large amount of money so that they can see if the bank teller is dishonest. The withdrawal is made in cash, and the victim gives the money to the con man. He advises that he will return it later in the day. The victim reports the crime when the con man does not show. Her motivation for participating comes from civic pride and a feeling of duty. Assisting the police or bank examiner is the right thing to do. It is extremely important to obtain information from the victim on the location where the con took place, vehicles used, any names that were used by the con team and complete physical descriptions. It is important to obtain this information quickly as the con artists tend to move geographically after a con has been perpetrated.

Confidence games generally require greed on the part of the victim. In the pigeon drop and three-card Monte, a group of con artists present a play that leads victims to believe that they will get something for nothing. All they have to do is participate. The con game is orchestrated, and even people who have common sense and intelligence can be duped. Typically the con involves the approach or conversation by the con team to the "mark" or victim, the offer of something for nothing and then getting the victim to physically give up his or her money.

Bank kiting is a con that is perpetrated upon the bank and involves setting up checking accounts and then removing the money so that the checks are no good. They then buy items with the worthless checks and leave the area with the goods. One of the latest types of crimes is one that involves identity theft. This occurs when a thief steals a credit card and then poses as the victim charging up all that he or she can until the card is cancelled. One of the most common methods in which a thief obtains your credit card number is by stealing the card or any documentation with the credit card number on it. Once thieves have the number then they can start to charge. Credit card carbon copies or receipts containing the number are commonly found in dumpsters behind department stores. Thieves know this and either go hunting through the dumpsters themselves or pay someone who will. Since the increase in the use of the Internet, thieves posing as representatives of Internet service providers routinely ask over the Internet for credit card numbers randomly. This results in untold thousands of dollars lost fraudulently. Credit cards are taken during burglaries, robberies, and by dishonest store clerks who fail to return the card. Prostitutes regularly steal from the wallets of their unsuspecting John's while engaged in their trade.

Identify four types of con games:

1. _____

2. _____

3. _____

4. _____

Who are commonly targeted for this type of crime?

_____

What does greed have to do with the con game, if anything?

_____

_____

_____

SCENARIO NUMBER ELEVEN:

The Home Invasion

An elderly woman is beaten and robbed in her house. During the robbery, her assailant rendered her unconscious. He may have presumed her to be dead. The attack occurred at 10:00 P.M. At 10:30 P.M., the victim's ATM card is used at her bank and fifty dollars is withdrawn. The security camera at the bank took several photographs of the suspect who was later arrested and convicted for attempted murder, robbery, uttering a forged document, and aggravated abuse of the elderly. These serious crimes were linked to the card and assisted in identifying the suspect in the case. Burglars, thieves, and murderers have been caught and prosecuted successfully based upon their possession and/or use of stolen credit cards. When a credit card is stolen, the thief normally attempts to copy the signature on the back. The actual signing of someone else's name on a document such as a check is known as forgery. Presenting the check to a bank teller or cashier is known as uttering a forged instrument. It is often difficult to prove forgery as the suspect normally does this in private. There is a great deal of evidence to prove uttering, which is normally done in public with witnesses present. In order to utter, there must be a person to receive the document. Common cases of forgery include such things as altering checks (adding zeros, e.g., $10.00 becomes $100.00). By forging the endorsement on the check or by using a fictitious name. Check washing is becoming a serious problem. A check that was cashed is recovered and then washed in chemicals that remove the ink from the signature and written sections. The chemicals leave the printed ink intact. Once dry, the forger has a blank check to write. In cases of forgery it is important to protect the evidence by keeping it intact. The documents must not be handled excessively and should be stored in a wrapper that is designed for the purpose. No marks should be made on the document; it should not be folded, bent, or stapled. A working copy should be made for the investigator. The original should be placed into evidence as any other evidence.

Identify four methods that thieves use to obtain credit cards:

1. _____

2. _____

3. _____

4. _____

1. What is the difference between forgery and uttering a forgery?

_____

_____

_____

2. What types of cases have been linked to credit card fraud and theft?

_____

_____

_____

3. How should suspected documents be handled?

_____

_____

4. What is identity theft?

_____

_____

5. How can people protect themselves from this type of crime?

_____

_____

A housewife at the grocery store writes a check and knows that there isn't enough money in the checking account to cover the check. She is intent on transferring funds to the account before the check clears. A week goes by, and she forgot to transfer funds to the account. The check bounces. Her bank returned the check to the grocery store for insufficient funds and charges her account thirty dollars for processing an insufficient funds check. The grocery store contacts the housewife and charges her an additional twenty-five-dollars fine for the returned check. The housewife then goes to the grocery store and pays the original amount plus the fine. Although the check she wrote was worthless, she did not have the criminal intent for being charged with a worthless check violation. Had she refused to make the check good, and the store pressed charges she could be charged with theft. It must be noted that people who accept checks from others as payment can get caught up in insufficient check problems through no fault of their own. It becomes a domino effect. There are cases when an employee of an organization, who has access to the company funds, generates a check to himself. This is done without the knowledge or consent of the company. This type of crime is known as embezzlement. It is one of the most common of the "white collar" crimes. The local church bookkeeper, treasurer, or clerk skims money off the top over a period of years and is caught when a new pastor with accounting experience conducts a surprise audit. Bank tellers who come up short and then disappear are also highly suspect in this type of crime. Sometimes the perpetrator initially thought that he or she was just "borrowing" some money and later forgot to pay it back. Many times it is done because the perpetrator believes that he or she is "owed" the money by the organization for all the extra work that he or she was never paid. The classic embezzler takes a large sum and is arrested when he or she attempts to start a new life. Sometimes gamblers, alcoholics, and drug addicts are in positions that give them access to funds. This should be no surprise to the company. A person who lives beyond his or her means and has personal problems resulting from lifestyle choices can also end up embezzling. Organizations who have in place appropriate accounting practices and who conduct background checks on the people to whom they trust funds with have a lower rate of this type of crime. On occasion, criminals attempt to cover up crimes by setting a fire to destroy the evidence. This happens with burglaries, embezzlements, and sometimes murder. The investigation of arson is difficult as this crime is normally done in private and a great deal of the evidence is destroyed as a result of the fire. If the building is on fire at the time officers arrive it is important that those adjourning buildings are evacuated and the fire department notified. Law enforcement officers must protect any scene suspected of arson. Fire marshals and trained arson investigators will normally conduct the investigation.

Identify the difference between an insufficient funds check and a worthless check case?

_____

_____

_____

_____

What are three professions or positions that are conducive to embezzlement?

1. _____

2. _____

3. _____

What are three rationalizations that embezzlers use to justify their crimes?

  1. _____

  2. _____

  3. _____

What are two reasons why embezzlers steal from their employers?

  1. _____

  _____

  2. _____

  _____

There are specific laws that protect archaeological sites and artifacts. There is a great deal of black market trade in these types of items. The fact that they are protected makes them more valuable to the people who desire to possess them. These artifacts include Indian burial mounds and associated sites, excavation sites that are being documented by anthropologists or historically significant areas that are protected by law.

SCENARIO NUMBER TWELVE:
The Burial Mound

You are patrolling in an area that has an Indian burial mound, which is protected by law. You observe two teenagers coming down off of the mound carrying an object. The object is a broken clay pot with a geometric design on the side. They relate that they found it on the top of the mound next to a small tree. As you detain the two, they advise that there is an older guy on the other side of the mound who has a pick ax and is digging up all kinds of stuff and sifting it through a screen. You call for another unit and advise the sergeant of the situation. The other unit locates the suspect on top of the mound with the excavation tools. The suspect has a station wagon with shovels and assorted other items and artifacts inside. The sergeant arrives and decides to call the crime scene technicians to document the scene.

1. What type of crime, if any, have the two teens committed?

_____

2. What type of crime has the man with the pick ax and screen committed?

_____

_____

3. When the man is taken into custody, what will happen to his vehicle and tools?

_____

_____

4. What is the motivation for someone to dig into a protected archaeological site?

_____

_____

5. Why is it important is it to enforce these laws?

_____

_____

The teenagers have committed a misdemeanor by trespassing on and removing an artifact from a protected site. The man has committed a felony because he actually dug into the site. Once the investigators interrogated the man, he implicated another person who contracted him to recover several items of interest to him. He is also guilty of a felony. The man who was digging into the mound may very possibly lose his car and all of the tools that he used in this crime through forfeiture.

SUMMARY

In this chapter, we discussed the different types of property crimes and the circumstances that generally surrounding them. We explored the types of theft victims and what information is necessary for a report to be completed. In vehicle theft, we identified circumstances that are reported as theft, which are not thefts. Vehicle identification procedures were discussed, as were indicators of stolen vehicles and sources of information available to law enforcement in regard to stolen vehicles. Finally, things that an officer should not do when investigating a stolen vehicle were considered.

This chapter went on to discuss the categories of burglars, types of burglaries, methods burglars use to enter structures, and procedures to follow when investigating a burglary. Next, the crime of fraud was discussed. Common types of con games and the components were identified as were the law enforcement response to these types of crimes. Credit card theft and fraud were defined. Methods criminals use to obtain credit cards was identified as were associated types of crimes which are linked to the theft. The two aspects of forgery were discussed, as were the most common types of forgery and investigative procedures to use when investigating forgery. The difference between a forged check, worthless check, and insufficient funds check were discussed. The crime of arson and procedures to follow when at a fire scene were discussed. The chapter next discussed embezzlement. The professions that are most likely to be involved in embezzlement were identified, as were the rationale of the criminals and the actual reasons as to why they steal. Finally, the crimes involved in the excavation and removal of artifacts from a protected archaeological site was discussed, as were the penalties associated.

CROSSWORD PUZZLE

Down

1. Entering with the intent to commit a crime
3. A burglar who is rarely, if ever, caught
6. Signing another person's name without his or her permission
7. To go door to door in order to ask if anyone witnessed anything related to a crime being investigated

Across

2. Stealing from a store
4. A site which is protected by law because of its historical relevance
5. A crime that occurs when someone is in a position of trust and steals that which he or she is entrusted to protect
8. A criminal set-up that plays upon the greed of people
9. A young burglar

Test Your Knowledge

For each multiple choice question select the best possible answer.

1. All of the following are examples of thefts except:
   a. burglary.
   b. shoplifting.
   c. retail.
   d. internal.

2. All of the following are examples of methods of identifying a vehicle except:
   a. license number.
   b. mileage of vehicle.
   c. vehicle identification number.
   d. engine number.

3. Indicators that a vehicle is stolen are:
   a. the ethnicity of the driver.
   b. tag is clean on a dirty car.
   c. the race of the driver.
   d. the gender of the driver.

4. Types of burglars include all of the following except:
   a. the drug addict.
   b. the professional.
   c. the semi-professional.
   d. the amateur.

5. Methods burglars use to gain entry include:
   a. kicking the front door in.
   b. entering through unlocked doors and windows.
   c. smashing out the sliding glass doors.
   d. shooting off a lock.

6. An officer going door-to-door in a neighborhood that has experienced a crime in order to obtain information is known as a:
   a. cotton.
   b. cloth.
   c. canvass.
   d. tweed.

7. One of the most common ingredients in a con game is:
   a. greed.
   b. generosity.
   c. fear.
   d. pride.

8. The average victim of a con artist is:
   a. young.
   b. unintelligent.
   c. elderly.
   d. middle-aged.

9. The actual signing of someone else's name on a document is known as:
   a. fraud.
   b. uttering a forgery.
   c. forgery.
   d. all of the above.

10. The embezzler's rationalization for his or her stealing include:
    a. he or she is just borrowing the money and will some day pay it back.
    b. the money is for a fresh start.
    c. "the company owes me the money."
    d. all of the above.

Death Investigations

Television, Hollywood, the media, and computerized games all present graphic demonstrations of death and dying. These presentations are made in such a manner as to inform or entertain. In the media, ratings are used to reflect how many people are watching. Some television stations are more graphic than others and are more aggressive towards victims. Asking a grieving mother what it feels like to lose her child, zooming in on a pool of blood on the ground and, if possible, getting a close-up of the body appeals to these types of reporters. If you ask them, they will tell you that the people have a right to know. Seeing trauma and scenes of horrific violence on a television screen or in a movie theater is shocking until it becomes so commonplace that it no longer affects the viewer. This desensitization of the viewer may make the scene less horrific and the results of this and its impact on society are the subject of many debates. Hollywood presented a motion picture in which a young FBI agent right out of the academy was part of a profiling team that was attempting to find and arrest a serial killer. In the film, she enters the darkened house of the suspect, turns a corner and finds a putrefied corpse in a bathtub. *This surprises her!*

In the real world:

1. she lacks the required experience to be working with the serial killer profiling team, and
2. she would never be entering a suspect's residence alone, and
3. the body in the tub would make itself known at least a block away from the house, and even if the house were sealed, she would be affected by it after entering the front door.

Hollywood has the visual aspects of horror but does not want to really gross out the audience. The real world does not have background music, editors, or stunt doubles.

In the real world, people get hurt and are devastated. One of the most difficult things a police officer has to do is to deliver the bad news that a loved one has died or been killed. There is no good way to do this. There is no way to feel good about a job well done. Looking at the faces of the people in shock, denial, and anger over the loss of someone close is a hard thing to do. The officer can't make it better or take it personally. Police officers and, specifically, homicide investigators lose a certain amount of sensitivity because of the nature of their work. This is not to say that they don't care. It is that they have learned to adapt to their environment by not getting emotionally involved with the cases that they work. If they became emotionally involved, they would be less effective and not able to do their best work.

A six-year-old girl was playing on the back steps of her house. She had a ribbon that she put around her neck. For some reason, she put the other end of the ribbon over the doorknob of the back door. The door swung open, and she hung off the side of the porch and strangled to death. Her family was eating lunch at the time of the incident and didn't hear anything. The investigator observed the child at the morgue. The child was approximately the same age as his children. When asked what he felt during the autopsy, he replied that the ligature marks around the neck were interesting as well as the fact that the child had been sexually molested. Both of these observations were important to the death investigation. Investigators must be able to separate their personal lives from their professional lives. The fact that this child was the same age as his does not enter into his mind except as a passing thought. The dead child is *work product*. The concept of work product allows the investigator to deal the horror of what he or she is observing by categorizing it under things that go with the job. Once the image or event is properly understood for what it is, the officer or investigator can function without undue emotional attachment. Police officers and investigators deal with human beings both dead and alive and sometimes in various stages of trauma. Looking at the dead child to this investigator was similar to looking at a dead adult, dead dog, or dead cat. His belief system allows him to work unimpeded with unnecessary emotional responses. He will focus on solving the crime. This investigator went home from the morgue, gave his wife and kids a hug, and sat down to dinner. At dinner there were no discussions about death or investigations, murder or mayhem.

What might happen to law enforcement officers or investigators who become emotionally attached to cases?

_____

_____

_____

How can they prevent becoming emotionally attached to cases?

_____

_____

Explain the concept of "work product" as it relates to law enforcement:

_____

_____

_____

SCENARIO NUMBER ONE:

The Death Investigation

It's Saturday morning at 7:00 A.M. You are dispatched to 911 Pine Street in reference to a deceased person. Upon arrival, the son of the deceased person greets you. He is visibly shaken and distraught. The paramedics are already inside the residence. You follow him inside, and seated in the living room in a recliner is an elderly man who the complainant advises is his father. The paramedics advise that the man is dead and has been for several hours. This determination is helpful, because there is no question as to whether the man is in need of CPR. This technique is only used when breathing and heartbeat have recently stopped. The complainant advised that his father was under the care of Dr. Smith for a chronic heart condition. As you look at the deceased, you notice his eyes are open, and it appears that he is staring at you. His head is lying against and to the right of the headrest. His eyes are dilated, and there is a thin opaque film over them. His mouth is slightly open, and his tongue is covering his lower teeth. He is not breathing. His skin is cool to the touch. His arm is stiff, and his position is fixed. On the lower side of his face, the skin has turned red as if he had been bruised or burned. His pants are soaked with urine, and there is a strong smell of feces. On the table next to his chair is an open bottle of heart medication. The medication has the deceased man's name and the name of his physician.

1. What do you do next?

_____

_____

2. Who do you notify? Why?

_____

_____

3. Identify the conditions that determine death in the case above. (How do you know he is dead?)

_____

_____

_____

4. How do you treat the relatives in this case?

_____

_____

_____

5. You feel as if you are going to be sick. What do you do?

_____

_____

In all cases of death, breathing and heartbeat stop, the pupils of the eyes dilate, and the body begins to cool to room temperature. The sphincter muscles relax and urine and feces can be released. As time passes, the eyes film over as they dry out. If you have ever been to a fish market, the eyes of fish do the same thing over time. The body begins to stiffen from the breakdown of enzymes and the accumulation of acid in the muscle tissue. This is known as *rigor mortis*. Rigor begins approximately two to four hours after death, is complete within six to twelve hours, and disappears within twenty-four to thirty-six hours. Rigor mortis can be accelerated from high fever, high environmental temperature, muscular activity, convulsions, and even fright. The blood in the body is no longer being pumped and gravity causes it to pool. This pooling causes the skin to turn red and appears to be a bruise or burn marks on the lower extremities. This is known as *postmortem lividity*. Lividity begins one-half hour to one hour after death, is well developed within three to four hours and is fixed within eight to twelve hours. As time passes, a breakdown of the body tissues from bacteria and chemical actions begins. This is known as putrefaction or decomposition. Decomposition begins at the abdomen and genitals as a greenish discoloration that turns darker with time.

Identify the time frames involved in:

Post mortem lividity_____

Rigor mortis _____

Name the conditions in which rigor mortis is accelerated:

1. _____

2. _____

3. _____

4. _____

5. _____

When you are driving you have no doubt encountered a dead animal on the side of the road. You may have noticed that the longer it is on the side of the road, the bigger it gets. This is from the gasses that form inside the animal. After a while, the gasses are released and the animal continues to decompose until there is just hair and some bones on the ground. The unpleasant smell is the result of this decomposition process. Insects assist in this process and can be valuable tools in determining the time of death. A blow-fly larva is a common insect found where decomposing animals are present. This type of insect takes a certain length of time to develop. Forensic scientists can determine time frames by identifying stages of development of the larva found on the body.

In the case of our deceased elderly man above, his doctor would undoubtedly sign his death certificate as to the cause of his death. No circumstances were present that would require the medical examiner to perform an autopsy. Regardless of the circumstance, the final decision on whether to perform an autopsy is made by the medical examiner. In this case, the individual was under a doctor's care and the cause of death was apparent. The medical examiner is ultimately responsible for all death investigations. Generally, as a criminal investigation is conducted by law enforcement, the medical examiner's investigators conduct a parallel investigation. This also depends upon the jurisdiction and local budget of the government. Some medical examiners work alone and have no staff and are severely limited. The autopsy is a protocol that is used to determine the cause of death. Even if a person is decapitated, an autopsy will be performed. By virtue of being a protocol, it is performed the same way on everyone, regardless of the circumstances. It is scientific, and the results render a great deal of information on the deceased. During an autopsy the medical examiner determines the official cause of death. Autopsies are generally required when a person dies as the result of any crime, accident, suicide, for no apparent reason, and when unattended by a physician. If a person dies in the custody of the police or in a prison, an autopsy is required. This is also the case if the person dies of a disease, injury, or toxic agent from employment or from a disease that constitutes a threat to public health. When a body is brought into the state without proper medical documentation, and when a body is to be cremated, dissected, or buried at sea, an autopsy is required. All the information that criminal investigators obtained relative to the cause of death must be shared with the medical examiner. Medical examiners are called to court regularly as the cause of death is extremely important in the prosecution of homicide cases.

1. What can insects reveal to forensic scientists about a body that is found in the woods?

_____

_____

2. What happens to people's eyes after they die?

_____

_____

3. Who determines the cause of death in all homicides?

_____

_____

4. What is postmortem lividity?

_____

_____

5. When is an autopsy necessary?

_____

_____

SUMMARY

In the first part of this chapter, we discussed the manner in which law enforcement officers respond to calls involving death. The most important technique that is used by those who work these types of cases and in this environment is to *not* become emotionally attached or involved in the case. To do so would be counterproductive and potentially harmful to the officer. Next we identified conditions, which determine death, and in what circumstances CPR should be implemented. The natural process of decomposition was presented, as were the various stages, signs, and time frames. Finally the role of the medical examiner was discussed as was the importance and requirements of the autopsy.

CROSSWORD PUZZLE

Down

1. The stiffening of the joints after death
2. The unlawful killing of another human being
3. A medical protocol used to determine cause of death
6. This is a perspective that allows investigators to remain detached from death scenes
7. This is what the pupils do after death
8. A common response to unexpected death
9. A common insect larvae found around decomposing animals

Across

4. One of the symptoms of a person in the initial stages of grief
5. This is where murder victims are taken
7. The natural breakdown of a human body after death
10. After death
11. The pooling of blood in a corpse

Test Your Knowledge

For each multiple choice question select the best possible answer.

1. For an investigator to be effective during the investigation of a death, he or she must remain:
   a. emotionally unattached.
   b. professional.
   c. cold and callous.
   d. a and b.

2. All of the following are conditions that determine death except:
   a. rigor mortis.
   b. decomposition.
   c. shallow breathing.
   d. fixation and dilation of pupils.

3. A general stiffening of the body caused by a breakdown of enzymes and the accumulation of acid in the muscles is known as:
   a. postmortem lividity.
   b. rigor mortis.
   c. postmortem rigidity.
   d. none of the above.

4. Body temperature begins to fall after death and eventually becomes:
   a. equal to the surroundings.
   b. colder than the surroundings.
   c. hotter than the surroundings.
   d. all of the above.

5. Rigor mortis can be accelerated by:
   a. high fever.
   b. high environmental temperature.
   c. fright.
   d. all of the above.

6. The discoloration caused by pooling of the blood in a body is know as:
   a. postmortem rigidity.
   b. postmortem lividity.
   c. postmortem rapidity.
   d. rigor mortis.

7. The breakdown of the body mass through bacterial and chemical action is know as:
   a. decomposition.
   b. rigor mortis.
   c. putrefaction.
   d. a and c.

8. Insect infestation found on bodies can be used to:
   a. help establish a motive.
   b. help establish a weapon.
   c. help establish time of death.
   d. help identify the murderer.

9. The person who determines the official cause of death is known as:
   a. the homicide investigator.
   b. the homicide technician.
   c. the medical examiner investigator.
   d. the medical examiner.

10. An autopsy is generally required when a person dies as the result of:
    a. a crime of violence.
    b. accident.
    c. suicide.
    d. all of the above.

CHAPTER 9

Sudden Infant Death Syndrome Procedures

One of the most disturbing calls that a law enforcement officer will ever answer is to investigate the death of a newborn baby. *Sudden infant death syndrome* (or *crib death*) is something that all new parents fear. The one consistent characteristic of SIDS is that there is no explanation for the death. Responding to a scene such as this can be troubling for the officer. It is at this time that he or she *must* be able to refrain from becoming emotionally attached to the case. A SIDS death investigation is best likened to a *homicide investigation with kid gloves*. This is a very serious investigation that is conducted with the purpose of discovering the cause of death. It must be conducted with extreme discretion. The parents are traumatized and are to be considered victims of the most horrible of circumstances. On the other hand, there have been unknown numbers of homicides that were misdiagnosed as SIDS. People in general don't want to believe that anyone would or could harm an infant. Unfortunately, there are people who kill children. They kill them through neglect and with full intent. Child abuse is alive and well in this country, and just like SIDS, it crosses all racial, ethnic, and socioeconomic boundaries. Once again, an investigator must remain emotionally unattached and be able to work the case efficiently and effectively. In the case of sudden infant death syndrome, all things that could have caused the death of the child must be eliminated prior to being given this cause of death. SIDS is the leading cause of death in infants under the age of one. Ninety percent of all SIDS deaths occur in infants under six months and the most common occurrence is between two and four months of age. Although it may be less common, these types of deaths occur in older babies as well. Males are more likely to die from SIDS than females. The occurrence of SIDS is approximately two in one thousand live births and is responsible for 85 percent of all sudden and unexpected post-neonatal infant deaths. Most of these types of deaths occur during the fall or winter months. Law enforcement is commonly called to the scene after the

99

paramedics have arrived and made the determination as to the use of CPR. If a law enforcement officer arrives prior to the paramedics, then he or she will have to make the determination as to CPR. Local policies and procedures will direct on these actions. The physical features of an infant who has died of SIDS includes changes in the skin appearance. This includes blue or gray coloration along with a dark redness resembling bruising or burned tissue. It is also common to find a frothy aspirate tinged with blood exiting the mouth or nose. Physically, there is nothing that distinguishes a SIDS death from other causes during the initial phases of the investigation. The investigator must be careful so that he or she does not jump to conclusions and decide that this is or is not a SIDS death.

What is the leading cause of death of infants under the age of one year?

_____

What is a SIDS death investigation best likened to?

_____

What time of the year typically has the most SIDS deaths?

_____

Why does an investigation have to be completed on every SIDS case?

_____

_____

SIDS almost always occurs while the infant is sleeping or believed to be sleeping. The infant is healthy prior to death but may have had a mild upper-respiratory infection or recent physical stress of some type. When the parent returns to the crib he or she finds the infant deceased. Although the child's head might be in the corner of the bed face down, this does not indicate suffocation.

SCENARIO NUMBER ONE:
SIDS Death

It's November 28, Thanksgiving Day. You just came on shift. Its 6:15 A.M., and you are dispatched to a disturbance call involving the paramedics who have responded to 611 Elm Street in reference to an infant who was having breathing problems. Upon your arrival, you are met by a paramedic who advises you that the baby is dead and has been so for approximately six hours. The baby is in the back bedroom in his crib. The firefighters who responded with the paramedics are attempting to calm the parents down. The parents are screaming and crying. The father of the child is becoming angry and yelling at the paramedic to perform CPR and bring his child back. The angry father looks at you and demands that you do something.

What do you do? Why?

_____

_____

_____

_____

SCENARIO NUMBER TWO:

SIDS Death

After you responded in a calm manner to the father that there is nothing that can be done for his child and that being upset with the paramedic is not going to help anyone, you summoned your sergeant and briefed him on the situation. He called out the investigators. Depending upon the time and day, the investigators could take as much as thirty minutes to respond.

What should you do while you are waiting for the investigators?

_____

_____

_____

_____

Anyone in crisis needs support. This support could come from their church, temple, or place of worship. If the parents have no affiliation, then a victim's advocate could be summoned. The parents or caregivers can demonstrate a whole range of emotional responses. This may include denial, anger, hysteria, withdrawal, intense guilt, or no response at all. The parents may make demands of the first responding officer or paramedics such as demanding CPR be performed or terminated, demanding to be alone with the infant, and wanting to know the cause of death. These questions could be made in a repetitive manner and the caregivers may even attempt to interfere with the paramedics or persons performing their duties.

SCENARIO NUMBER THREE:

SIDS Death

While you are waiting, a relative drives up in his car and screeches to a stop. He runs to the door and demands to know "what the hell is going on." He has been drinking and appears to be intoxicated. He demands to go inside the house and see his sister. As the moments go by, he becomes more and more agitated and profane.

1. What kinds of problems can this person cause?

_____

_____

_____

2. What are your responsibilities at this crime scene?

_____

_____

_____

3. What are you going to do now?

_____

_____

_____

4. What impact could this person have on the victims?

_____

_____

5. Is arrest your only solution? Is it the best solution?

_____

_____

The upset relative must be brought under control immediately. His actions have the potential of causing the victims more harm, interfering with the investigation, and his intoxicated state adds to the unpredictability of his behavior. It is important to remove him from the scene. It is imperative that this is done with great tact. The last thing that the victims need is to have a relative arrested for disorderly conduct in front of them.

Choking, child abuse, disease, heredity, suffocation, overheating, immunizations, or vomiting do not cause SIDS. SIDS is the cause of death, and thereby has no understandable physical cause. If the child suffocated or was the victim of abuse, then those would be the causes of death. The cause of SIDS is and remains unknown.

Once the investigators arrived your duties change to one of security. The investigators will introduce themselves to the parents and explain the investigation process including the need for an autopsy. This is done in a calm and caring manner. The investigator has to use great care in explaining the need for autopsy. The purpose of the autopsy is to determine cause of death. The law requires this procedure. Until an autopsy is performed, the cause will remain unknown. Any direction given to the parents must be clear and presented with concern for both the parents and the crime scene. The parents must be reassured that there was nothing that they could have done to prevent the death. If permissible, a parent or caregiver should be allowed to accompany the infant when transported. One of the first observations and notations the investigator must make is the location of the infant. Was he or she in the crib, on the bed, or floor? Any objects found in the vicinity of the infant must be documented, as well as the conditions present in the room. Did the room have a foul odor or high temperature? Special notation must be made of any medications present. In questioning the parents or caregivers, the investigator must use non-leading, open-ended questions such as "what happened?" The investigator's report should involve responses to the questions, who found the infant, what was done when the infant was found, was the body moved, what time was the infant last seen alive, what was the health of the infant, and how was the infant's disposition that day? It is important to gather these facts and document the answers so that all personnel involved have the answers and are not repeating the same questions and causing the parents or caregivers additional stress.

SCENARIO NUMBER FOUR:

The Suspicious Death

It's Tuesday, 11:00 P.M. on December 12th, and you have been dispatched to 607 Pine Street in reference to a young babysitter who discovered that the infant in her care was not breathing in its crib. A paramedic who advises that the infant is deceased meets you at the front door. As you enter the house, you notice the strong smell of sandalwood incense. There are posters of marijuana and drug-related materials on the walls. There is a black light attached to the wall over the living room sofa. There are six empty beer bottles on the coffee table and two half-full ones with condensation on the outside. There is a large bong on the table. As you enter the nursery, you notice that the infant is lying in a pool of vomit. The vomit smells strongly of beer. In the corner of the crib is a baby bottle with an amber colored liquid inside. There is a small amount of foam on the surface of the liquid.

1. Do you believe that this is a SIDS case? Why or why not?

_____

_____

_____

2. Do you think that the babysitter was alone? Why?

_____

_____

_____

3. What information does the environment provide for you in this case?

_____

_____

_____

4. Should you allow the caretakers in the room where the baby is? Why or why not?

_____

_____

5. What is the significance of the bottle in the crib? How should it be treated?

_____

_____

SCENARIO NUMBER FIVE:

The Suspicious Death

As you enter the kitchen, you observe the babysitter, seated at the kitchen table. She has her head in her hands and is crying. As she looks up, you observe that her eyes are red and bloodshot and the pupils are extremely dilated. You ask her what happened? She advised that the parents of the child are away on a motorcycle trip for a few days. She related that the baby wouldn't quit crying so her boyfriend gave him some beer. At the autopsy, it was determined that the child died as the result of toxic levels of alcohol.

1. Should the babysitter be read her Miranda warning?

_____

_____

2. Do you believe that she is most probably high? Why?

_____

_____

3. What charges should be made against the babysitter? Why?

_____

_____

4. What charges should be made against babysitter's boyfriend? Why?

_____

_____

5. Do you believe that this was an intentional act or an accident?

_____

_____

SCENARIO NUMBER SIX:
The Suspicious Death

After work you go home. In the night, you are disturbed by constant dreams about the child who was murdered. You don't get much sleep. The next day you go to work, but can't seem to concentrate. Your mind keeps going back to the scene of that child in the crib. You start to have a short temper with your co-workers. You really don't want to socialize with anyone of them. You just want to be left alone. As time goes by, you begin calling in sick and staying in bed.

What is happening to you?

_____

_____

_____

_____

What can be done to help you?

_____

_____

_____

_____

There are many reasons why officers might start to experience the effects of stress. It is not uncommon for officers who have experienced all kinds of horrible sights on the job to be relatively unaffected until they work a case involving an infant. This is especially true if they have children of their own. Officers may begin to identify with the parents in the case. They may start to doubt their abilities and become troubled that they could have done something to revive the infant. Officers in this situation need to exercise, get rest, and not work overtime if possible. They need to research

SIDS and obtain feedback and educational materials from SIDS parent groups. They may need professional counseling and, if their problems relate to a singular event, they may request a critical incident stress debriefing if available. The support groups for parents who have been affected by SIDS are easily located. Nationally the SIDS Alliance number is 1-800-221-SIDS. All officers should be able to provide a phone number to victims of this devastating occurrence.

SUMMARY

In this chapter, we discussed the epidemiology of SIDS. Age distribution, population distribution, as well as the seasonal distribution were identified. The physical features of the SIDS infant were identified, as were the circumstances often associated with a SIDS death. We discussed actions that could cause injury or death that are not associated with SIDS such as child abuse and choking. The responsibilities of the first responding officer were discussed as were suggested methods providing support to the parents or caregivers. The various emotional responses of parents in this type of crisis were discussed. Observations that are required as part of the general investigation were identified as were methods of questioning the witnesses. Finally, the possible impact on the officer responding to this type of scene was discussed and suggestions for appropriate resolution were identified.

CROSSWORD PUZZLE

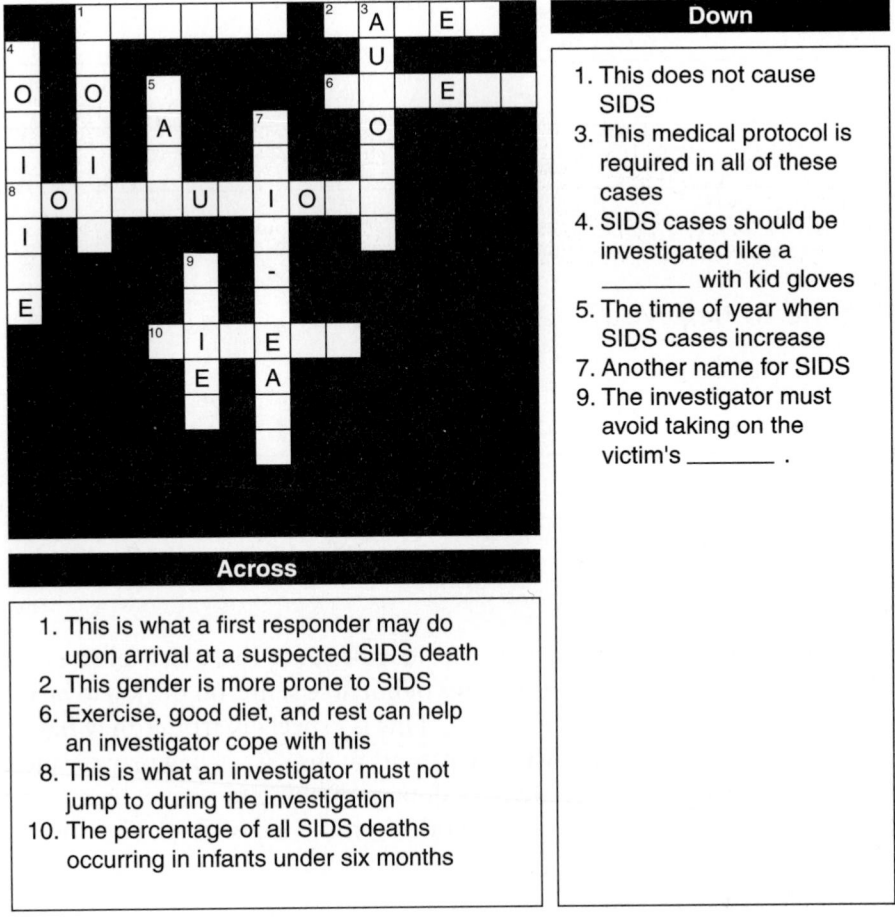

Down

1. This does not cause SIDS
3. This medical protocol is required in all of these cases
4. SIDS cases should be investigated like a _____ with kid gloves
5. The time of year when SIDS cases increase
7. Another name for SIDS
9. The investigator must avoid taking on the victim's _____ .

Across

1. This is what a first responder may do upon arrival at a suspected SIDS death
2. This gender is more prone to SIDS
6. Exercise, good diet, and rest can help an investigator cope with this
8. This is what an investigator must not jump to during the investigation
10. The percentage of all SIDS deaths occurring in infants under six months

Test Your Knowledge

For each multiple choice question select the best possible answer.

1. The sudden unexpected death of an apparently healthy infant usually under the age of one year, which remains unexplained after a complete medical history, death scene investigation and postmortem examination, is known as:
   a. SIDS.
   b. CHIDS.
   c. PEDS.
   d. none of the above.

2. _____% of all SIDS deaths occur in infants less than six months of age.
   a. 90
   b. 80
   c. 70
   d. 60

3. SIDS occurs at a rate of approximately _____/_____ live births
   a. 10/1,000
   b. 3/5,000
   c. 2/1,000
   d. 2/10,000

4. A greater number of SIDS deaths occur in:
   a. spring.
   b. summer.
   c. fall and winter.
   d. none of the above.

5. The gender death ratio among SIDS victims is:
   a. more females than males.
   b. more males than females.
   c. exactly the same.
   d. no one knows.

6. Actions which may cause illness, death, or injury include:
   a. child abuse or neglect.
   b. contagious disease.
   c. suffocation.
   d. all of the above.

7. A SIDS investigation should be done:
   a. as any other death or homicide investigation.
   b. with the object of making an arrest.
   c. with great care and compassion for the parents.
   d. only if foul play is suspected.

8. Non-leading and open-ended questions that an investigator may use include all of the following except:
   a. "Did you kill the baby?"
   b. "What happened?"
   c. "Who found the infant and where?"
   d. "Had the infant been sick?"

9. All of the following are potential emotional responses of parents who have lost a child in a SIDS death except:
   a. anger.
   b. denial.
   c. laughter.
   d. hysteria.

10. Some of the strategies for decreasing the impact of stress on an officer may include all of the following except:
    a. exercise.
    b. adequate diet and rest.
    c. professional counseling or critical incident stress debriefing.
    d. getting drunk.

Crimes Against Persons Preliminary Investigation

Crimes against persons are the most serious crimes encountered by law enforcement. This class of crime includes robbery, sex crimes, and homicide. Most of the crimes against persons involve violence or threat of violence.

SCENARIO NUMBER ONE:

The Sexual Battery

You are on patrol. Shortly after midnight you observe a female staggering out from the wooded area behind a convenience store. She collapses next to the building. As you approach, you observe that she is covered with dirt and her clothes are torn and in disorder. She has fresh bruises on her face as if she had been beaten. She tells you that she was raped in the woods and just wants to go home.

1. What is your first responsibility at this scene?

_____

_____

_____

2. What is your second responsibility?

_____

_____

3. What problems could your victim be experiencing?

_____

_____

4. Your victim wants to go home. Should you take her there? Why or why not?

_____

_____

_____

5. What could you do to make the victim more comfortable?

_____

_____

_____

After you summoned medical assistance for your victim and advised the sergeant of your situation, your thoughts should be focused upon some of the other needs of this person. She is experiencing a very well-founded fear. She may even be going into shock. She is afraid that you and the other officers will not be sympathetic and may even be judgmental. She is embarrassed and feels that she will be humiliated further in court. She is very concerned about retaliation by the perpetrator and does not feel safe. These feelings are aggravated by the fear that she may have contacted a communicable disease or AIDS. In many cases, she will want to go home, get cleaned up, and go to bed.

There are two things that a good police officer must have. They are common sense and compassion. Without common sense, the officer will be ineffective. Lacking compassion, the officer will be destructive. This victim needs to know that she is safe. The officer must be sensitive and humane. He or she must be able to calm down the victim and begin to obtain information so that a bulletin can be issued for the suspect. If possible, the location of the scene must be found, secured, and investigated. The officer must expect that the victim may be reluctant to cooperate because she is scared. It is very important to be patient and sensitive to the victim's needs. The officer must ask the victim for her assistance in this case and reassure her that the officer is there to help. It must be explained that her assistance can help the police put this criminal away. She should be informed that sex offenders often repeat their crimes and that she can help to stop him before he re-offends. The officer should make the victim feel that she is in control. The procedures of the investigation including the medical exam should be explained to her. As the case progresses and witnesses are identified, they should be interviewed separately.

Name five reasons why sexual battery is not reported:

1. _____

2. _____

3. _____

4. _____

5. _____

Name four ways an officer's attitude can assist in the investigation:

1. _____

2. _____

3. _____

4. _____

When a victim is being interviewed the officer must be extremely careful in how he or she asks questions. The last thing that an officer wants to do is to make the victim feel as if she is being judged. Questions such as:

> *"What were you doing down here dressed like that?"*
> *"Did you experience an orgasm or enjoy the act?"*
> *"Do you have a large number of sex partners?"*
> *"How large was your attacker's penis?"*
> *"Are you willing to take a lie detector test?"*

are absolutely inappropriate to ask of a victim and will result in the victim becoming hostile and uncooperative. How would you feel if you were a victim and the police doubted your story or made inappropriate remarks? If you have difficulty relating to the victim in this type of crime, then you should think how you would like your sister or mother to be treated in similar circumstances. There are questions that need to be asked of the victim to assist in the prosecution of the case. Some of these questions are embarrassing to the victim. Interviews with the victim should always be done in private. It is best if the investigator has a sexual battery checklist or form to fill out while interviewing the victim. This is important for three reasons. First, the checklist or form gives consistency to sex crimes investigation. Second, it is a valuable tool to assist the investigator in remembering to ask all of the questions required. And third and probably most importantly, the use of a form to ask these questions keeps the victim from thinking that the investigator is interrogating her or getting a cheap thrill by making up questions to ask. Everyone is used to filling out forms. The form in this case is asking the questions, not the investigator. The investigator should have a checklist that includes:

1. The time frame of the attack, location, and exact nature of the attack
2. The level of force and weapon used

3. The verbal behavior of the perpetrator

4. The identity of witnesses and an accurate description of any property stolen from the victim

5. A detailed description of the suspect

6. A detailed description of the victim

Documentation in all crimes is important. In the sexual battery investigations, the observations of the officer must be properly detailed and are crucial to the successful prosecution of the case. The officer must document the condition of the victim's clothing, general condition of the victim's face and hair. Exact physical descriptions of any bruises, scratches, cuts or injuries received during the attack are extremely important. Photographs of these injuries are helpful to the investigation. These photographs should be taken with the permission of the victim. If the injuries are in a location other than arms or face and require disrobing, an officer of the same gender should be assigned to document the injury. Under no circumstances should any officer attempt to conduct a medical examination. This examination is a medical-legal protocol and is normally conducted by a physician or nurse practitioner. The investigator should explain the necessity of the medical examination to the victim and stress the importance of the recovery of evidence from this exam. The officer must remember that injuries are not always present and not all victims appear the same. Many victims are coerced into submission by the size or threatening behaviors of the attacker.

Name three questions that should not be asked of a sexual battery victim:

1. _____

2. _____

3. _____

Identify five questions that you would ask the victim:

1. _____

2. _____

3. _____

4. _____

5. _____

Identify three items that an officer should look for when documenting the physical condition of a victim:

1. _____

2. _____

3. _____

SCENARIO NUMBER TWO:

The Robbery

It's Thursday night at 10:00 P.M. It has been a quiet night, and nothing eventful has occurred. All of a sudden, the dispatcher tones out a serious call. As you listen she refers to your zone and advises that the convenience store on First and Pine has just been robbed. You determine the fastest route and advise dispatch that you are responding.

There are three styles of robberies. The *ambush* is the one associated with a common mugging in a park. A situational victim is one who wanders down a path in the park and is ambushed by the robber who lays in wait. A *selective* robbery is one where the victims are selected as the preferred target. The target is selected based on several criteria. One selected group is intoxicated people. When people who are under the influence get robbed, they have difficulty remembering descriptions of their attackers. Senior citizens are another group that is targeted because they do not offer a physical threat to the robber. Prostitutes and persons engaged in the drug trade are targeted because they are not likely to report crimes to the police. Homosexuals in public bathrooms are another group that is hesitant to report crimes. The *planned* robbery is the one that is most associated with banks and retail operations such as convenience stores.

As you pull up to the convenience store, you advise dispatch that you are on the scene. You are careful to park your patrol car off to the side of the store and approach with great caution. Once you determine that the perpetrator is not on the scene, you enter the store and immediately check on the well-being of the clerk. If necessary, you summon rescue and have the victim treated. You advise the sergeant that your scene requires crime scene technicians. After conducting a preliminary interview of the victim, you initiate a Be on Lookout (BOLO) or bulletin with the description of the suspect and vehicle, and you secure the scene. It is important that you lock the door. This prevents unauthorized persons from gaining access to the crime scene and keeps your witnesses inside. You separate witnesses and interview each alone.

In the case of a bank robbery, the entire area would have to be sealed off and the FBI would have to be notified. The area would also be sealed off in the event of a homicide, an additional crime such as sexual battery, or if some other serious injury resulted in addition to the robbery. If the perpetrator spent an extended period of time at the scene, the investigators may want the scene sealed off for processing.

As you interview the store clerk, you are careful to obtain a complete description of the suspect(s), weapon(s) and manner in which the suspects acted just prior to the robbery. It is important to note if restraints were used and if the suspect(s) made demands. How the weapon was carried and displayed is extremely important, as is the exact wording that the suspect(s) used during the robbery. Notation should be made of all property taken along with serial numbers if available. After you finish your preliminary report, you brief the investigators and go back in service.

Name the three styles of robbery:

1. _____

2. _____

3. _____

Identify six common targets of robbery:

1. _____

2. _____

3. _____

4. _____

5. _____

6. _____

Identify three situations in which the area should be completely sealed off:

1. _____

2. _____

3. _____

List the first four procedures to follow upon arrival at a robbery scene:

1. _____

2. _____

3. _____

4. _____

Identify four items that should be included in the preliminary robbery report:

1. _____

2. _____

3. _____

4. _____

SCENARIO NUMBER THREE:

The Homicide

It's 2:15 A.M. Sunday morning, and you receive a tone out of a possible shooting in the parking lot of Joe's Bar. Upon your arrival, a crowd has gathered around a man who is lying on the ground with a large gunshot wound to his forehead. Witnesses advise that Harvey Frollic and the deceased were both drunk and arguing about a pool game. They went outside into the parking lot, and one witness advised that Harvey pulled out a gun and shot the victim "right between the eyes" and then fled in his red pickup truck. The paramedics arrive on the scene and pronounce the victim dead. As you are talking to witnesses, two other officers arrive. One witness shouts, "there he is now" and points to a red pickup truck driving slowly in front of the bar. You advise the other two officers who initiate a felony stop and secure the suspect. The investigators arrive on the scene, and you brief them and assist in obtaining all of the statements from the witnesses.

The patrol officer is normally the first one on the scene of a homicide. The patrol officer may assist in the preliminary investigation at the direction of the investigators. If a patrol officer questions a suspect and reads him a Miranda warning and the suspect asks for an attorney, the patrol officer has taken away from the investigators the opportunity to interview the suspect in more conducive surroundings. This behavior may jeopardize the case. The most important duties the patrol officer has in this type of crime is to secure and preserve the crime scene and witnesses, take accurate field notes, and await direction from the investigators. Many times the officer is responding to some other call, which turns out to be a homicide. Once it is determined to be a major crime such as a homicide the investigators will be notified and the scene is frozen until their arrival.

Disturbance calls and domestic problem calls can easily escalate into homicide. Officers must always approach these calls with extreme caution as the suspect may still be on the scene.

All dead body cases must be treated as potential homicides until proven otherwise. It is extremely important to use universal precautions (rubber gloves, etc.) when around body fluids and blood.

Name three concerns that an officer should have when approaching a dead body:

1. _____

2. _____

3. _____

How should all dead body cases be treated?

_____

_____

How can you protect yourself against possible hazardous materials associated with a dead body?

_____

_____

_____

ASSAULT AND BATTERY

As you remember, the difference between assault and battery consists of the threat of physical violence (assault) and the actual commission of the physical violence (battery).

SCENARIO NUMBER FOUR:

The Bar Fight

It's Monday night at 11:00 P.M. You are once again dispatched to a disturbance at Joe's Bar. Upon your arrival, an individual who is holding a bloody handkerchief over his nose meets you in the parking lot. He advises that Larry Frolic (Harry's brother) was drunk inside and punched him in the nose. The victim further stated that Larry was upset about his brother getting arrested. He knew that the victim was one of the witnesses in the case and punched him without provocation. Along with the victim was a barmaid who substantiated the victim's story (probable cause established). You made sure that you questioned her away from the victim (identify and separate witnesses).

After you summoned the paramedics to check on your victim, you request a backup unit to assist.

Your backup has just arrived, what should you do now?

_____

_____

_____

After you received a sworn statement from the victim and witness (detailed information about what happened), you and your backup unit approach the bar entrance. You asked both the victim and witness about possible weapons on the suspect, and they responded that he was unarmed as far as they knew. As you enter the bar, the suspect's back is to you. He is leaning on the bar talking to a woman sitting next to him. You and your backup quickly secure him at the bar and handcuff him. If he had left through the back door, you would have issued a BOLO. You know that you have a good battery case, but what about other criminal charges? The victim is a material witness in a homicide case against his brother. The reason that the victim was battered is because of his being a witness. If you are not sure, you should call the sergeant and ask for advice. Witness intimidation is a felony in most jurisdictions and might be an appropriate additional charge in this case.

Identify four procedures to follow upon arrival at an assault and battery scene:

1. _____

2. _____

3. _____

4. _____

SCENARIO NUMBER FIVE:

Spouse Abuse

While you were at Joe's Bar, the barmaid asked some legal advice about her younger sister. She was concerned about her sister being beaten up by her husband. She stated that yesterday while she was visiting her sister, she noticed that she had a black eye and some bruises around her neck. Her sister told her that she was late getting dinner on the table, and her husband grabbed her around the neck and started to choke her and then punched her in the eye. The waitress further advised that when she was talking to her sister, her husband came home and told her to leave and that she wasn't welcomed in their home. The waitress gave you the address and asked if you would help her younger sister. After you booked in Larry Frollic at the jail, you went over to the address that the waitress had given to you.

1. How dangerous is this type of call?

_____

_____

2. What could you do to reduce the level of danger to yourself?

_____

_____

3. Based upon the sister's testimony, do you have probable cause for an arrest?

_____

4. Do family members occasionally exaggerate the facts of a case such as this?

_____

5. If nothing is done to intervene, what is the likelihood of extreme harm or death to a person in this type of relationship?

_____

_____

As you got out of your unit, you heard a man's voice yelling and glass breaking. You called dispatch and advised of your location and the nature of your call. The sergeant advised that he was rolling your way. You knock on the door, and the yelling stops. You hear a woman's voice sobbing and the man telling her to shut up. As you knock on the door again, you notice the sergeant exiting his car and approaching. As you attempt to knock again, the door opens and a man asks, "What the hell do you want?" You ask to see his wife, and he says she is in bed. As you look inside the house you see his wife standing in the hallway. You ask the man to step aside and stand next to the sergeant. You ask the woman if you can come in, and she says yes. You observe that the woman has a black eye and a fresh hand imprint on her face. She advises that her husband has beaten her. The sergeant hand-cuffs the woman's husband, and he is secured in the back of your patrol car. You get written state-ment from the victim and give her information on resources available to her as well as procedures that she can use to get a restraining order. You stand by while she calls her sister to come and stay with her.

Once again, you are on your way to the county jail. Domestic violence does not have to be wit-nessed by the officer in order for an arrest to be made. When an officer has probable cause to believe that domestic violence has occurred, in most jurisdictions he or she has the authority to arrest with-out a warrant. Most domestic violence calls involve batteries of some type. It is important for the officer to understand the dynamics of these relationships and not become disillusioned when the victim has the perpetrator move back in and later the cycle of abuse continues.

CHILD ABUSE

Child abuse is a type of crime that can arouse a great deal of emotional response. Many officers have difficulty working these types of cases. Once again, it is extremely important that the officer remain professionally detached and not let emotions get in the way of doing his or her job.

SCENARIO NUMBER SIX:
The Neglected Child

It's Tuesday, you've just started day shift, and it's 6:30 A.M. As you are attempting to reacquaint your-self with working in the daylight, you observe what appears to be a very young child sitting next to a busy roadway with a box of crackers. The child is wearing only a pair of dirty underpants. His face is dirty, and he appears not to have been bathed for a number of days. The house that the child is sit-ting in front of is unkempt. The grass is overgrown, the house is in need of paint, and an old car is sitting on blocks in the front yard. The front door is open with the remnants of a screen door hang-ing from the hinges. You stop your vehicle and get out. You approach the child and pick him up. You bring him up to the porch and knock on the door. The smell of the house is offensive. After a few minutes, you knock again. A woman who was obviously asleep has awakened to answer the door. The woman sees her son and starts to yell obscenities at him. She grabs him by the arm and pulls him inside.

The primary concern of a law enforcement officer when investigating possible child abuse or neglect is the protection of the child. The Department of Children and Families investigates child abuse and acts as co-investigator to the police. This is an important relationship. If children need to be removed from a house, DCF is equipped with the resources to take them and place them in foster care. It is crucial that child abuse investigations are carefully coordinated between the police and DCF. Working together prevents possible conflict, redundant investigation processes, and wasted time.

As you are talking to the woman, you notice the smell of alcoholic beverages about her person. You inquire about how much she has been drinking, and she tells you: "That's none of your business." She then says "Thanks for bringing my kid back inside. I'll keep a better watch on him so it doesn't happen again." With that she says "good-bye" and shuts the interior door.

What should you do now? Why?

_____

_____

_____

What are the observations that you made that lead you to your decision?

_____

_____

There are cues that an officer needs to look for when investigating child abuse. Physical signs of abuse include suspicious bruises, welts, burns, or unusual fractures. Any child can have a bruise or a fracture. If there are multiple injuries in various stages of healing or if the injury is in an unusual location on the body, then the injury should be considered suspect. The actions or behavior of a child can also be tell-tale. A child who doesn't want to go home, is afraid of adults, or scared of his or her own parents can also be a possible indicator. Once again the totality of the circumstance must be looked at rather than an individual indicator. When talking to the parents of a suspected abused child some unusual traits may be observed. If parents demonstrate a great deal of immaturity, refer to the child as being evil or a "bad seed," or advises that they were abused as a child, the investigator should be concerned. If a parent attempts to conceal the injury of a child or to protect a person who caused the injury, the investigator should be extremely suspicious.

Child neglect is a form of abuse that is equally dangerous and damaging to children. Some indicators of neglect include the child who is constantly hungry, constantly lacking supervision, or has unattended medical or physical problems or needs such as open sores or wounds. A child who is always begging or stealing food, falling asleep in school, or engaging in delinquent acts also indicates possible neglect. Unsupervised children often get in trouble for stealing and criminal mischief.

Identify three observations of a physical nature that possibly indicates child abuse:

1. _____

2. _____

3. _____

List three behavioral observations, which may indicate child abuse:

1. _____

2. _____

3. _____

Identify three characteristics of abusive parents:

1. _____

2. _____

3. _____

Identify three indicators of child neglect:

1. _____

2. _____

3. _____

Identify three behaviors that may indicate child neglect:

1. _____

2. _____

3. _____

Sexual Abuse

Sexual abuse is one of the most horrible forms of child abuse. Some of the physical indicators of sexual abuse of a child include such things as venereal disease. Children as young as six months old have been treated for venereal disease. A child who has difficulty walking or sitting may have been sexually abused if there is no *reasonable explanation*. The child may simply have a straddle injury from a bicycle accident. Unexplainable bruises, bleeding from the external genitalia, rips or tears of vaginal or anal tissues are extremely suspect for sexual abuse.

Behavioral indicators of sexual child abuse include such conduct as acting out in a sexual manner that is not *age appropriate*. Children may play doctor, but the concept of oral sex would not come to them without witnessing or being a party to such events. A child who is unwilling to change for gym or participate in physical activities may be shy or withdrawn or possibly could have been sexually abused. The child who is extremely withdrawn, engages in a great deal of fantasy, or acts infantile in his or her behavior may be the victim of sexual abuse. Withdrawing is a common defense mechanism for a victim who is powerless over his or her attacker in these kinds of cases. The victims withdraw into themselves for protection. They may invent a fantasy place to go. The child may appear to be mentally retarded, sitting in a fetal position, rocking back and forth and not responding to outside stimulus.

In one case, an eight-year-old girl in school lifted up her dress, pulled down her underwear, and began to masturbate in front of the class. The child's teacher immediately called the police and the Department of Children and Families child abuse hotline 1-800-962-2873. Although the names may differ, every state has a department with similar responsibilities as the Department of Children and Families. The police officer took the initial report that included the child's name, age, sex, ethnicity, and address as well as the name of the person who is responsible for the child's welfare. A written confirmation report must be sent to the Department of Children and Families within forty-eight hours. The initial concerns of the officer investigating this case included determining the validity of the complaint, the amount of risk to the child at the home, if removal from the home was warranted, who was responsible for the abuse as well as the location and identification of any witnesses. During the investigation, it was discovered that her prostitute mother and an assortment of men had sexually abused the child since she was five years old. This woman abused the child sexually daily. The child was diagnosed as having two types of venereal disease. This information came directly from the child's testimony.

Prior to interviewing a child it is important to determine the child's ability to explain what happened and demonstrate an understanding of the difference between truth and lies. The age of the child has a great deal to do with this determination. In extremely young children, this can be problematic. A trained professional from the Child Protection Team should be used to interview if at all possible. The Child Protection Team is a group comprised of law enforcement, prosecutors, doctors, and social workers from the Department of Children and Families who actively participate in the investigation and prosecution of child abuse cases. The impact of the interview upon the child and the possible retaliation by a parent should always be considered when interviewing a child. An investigator who is interviewing a child victim should attempt to gain the child's confidence. He or she should not talk down to the child or use terms that the child would not understand. It is extremely important for the investigator not to side with the parents and instead to allow the child to describe the events in his or her own words. Even though this is a child victim, the investigator should explain the sequence of the prosecution. "What happens next?" is the question in the minds of all victims involved in the criminal justice system. In this case, the child was eight years old and was articulate and able to describe the abuse in great detail. This victim was immediately placed in foster care. One day, the foster care mother discovered the child performing sexual acts upon her nine-year-old son. The prostitute/mother subsequently confessed and pled guilty to capital sexual battery and was given ten years in prison. The court terminated her parental rights. The teacher who reported this case was operating under a legal mandate to report suspected child abuse or neglect. Medical personnel, mental health professionals, social workers, spiritual healers, day care workers, foster care or institutional workers, and all law enforcement officers are required to report suspected child abuse or neglect under penalty of law.

SCENARIO NUMBER SEVEN:
The Child in the Window

You are dispatched to a house in reference to a child in need of supervision. Upon your arrival you observe a filthy baby sitting in the window of a dilapidated old house. You announce yourself and knock on the door. As you look in the screen-less window, you are greeted with an incredible stench of what can only be decaying garbage and feces. You determine that there is no one home. The child is approximately three years old.

What do you do?

_____

_____

_____

_____

If the physical environment poses a threat to the child or there is maltreatment of the child or the potential of maltreatment that could result in permanent damage to the child's body or mind, then the officer must take an action to safeguard the child. Many times the family history will include prior incidents or allegations of abuse. The Department of Children and Families will know this history. The child in the window was turned over to the Department of Children and Families workers after a telephone report was made to the Department of Children and Families. The Department of Children and Families had an active file on this household. The confirmation report was sent, and the child was placed in foster care. An arrest warrant was requested for the mother who was later found intoxicated in a bar down the street.

Identify three physical indicators of possible sexual abuse:

1. _____

2. _____

3. _____

Identify three behavioral indicators of possible sexual abuse:

1. _____

2. _____

3. _____

List six occupations that are required by law to report child abuse:

1. _____

2. _____

3. _____

4. _____

5. _____

6. _____

Name three concerns that investigators should have when investigating child abuse:

1. _____

2. _____

3. _____

Identify three guidelines to follow when interviewing a child:

1. _____

2. _____

3. _____

SUMMARY

We began this chapter with the examination of the crime of sexual battery. We identified the reasons why sexual battery is not reported, as well as procedures to follow when responding to sexual batteries. Later we discussed the ways an officer's attitude can assist in the investigation and identified questions not to ask as well as information that must be obtained from the victim in this type of case. Case documentation and observations about the victim were also discussed. Next, the crime of robbery was discussed. The types and common targets of robbery were identified, as were the situations in which an area should be completely sealed off. The procedures used in responding to a robbery were identified, as were the items to be included in the preliminary robbery report. The crime of homicide was discussed next. The concerns of officers in the response of homicide cases were identified, as were safety issues. The differences between assault and battery were discussed, as were procedures to follow upon arrival to an assault and battery case. Domestic violence issues were identified, as were law enforcement arrest requirements. The issues surrounding child abuse finished the chapter. The cues that an officer may observe which may indicate child abuse and characteristics of abusive parents were identified, as were physical and behavioral indicators of child neglect and sexual abuse were discussed. The reporting requirements in child abuse cases were also identified.

CROSSWORD PUZZLE

Down

1. Intentional physical and mental injury inflicted upon a child
3. A sexual battery victim should be made to feel that she is in
4. Officers sometimes have to convince victims to do this
8. A type of robbery where the attacker jumps out of the bushes

Across

1. _____ along with common sense is essential for police officers to be effective
2. _____ violence is a battery between spouses
5. The unlawful touching or striking of another human being
6. An old term once used for sexual battery
7. The verbal threat of bodily harm
9. This is what officers must do to a crime scene to keep people out
10. The taking of something of value from someone by force
11. This is what all cases involving dead bodies must be treated as

Test Your Knowledge

1. All of the following are reasons that sexual battery is not reported except:
   a. the victim is embarrassed.
   b. the victim enjoyed the experience.
   c. the victim fears reprisal by the assailant.
   d. the victim feels that the officers will be unsympathetic.

2. When responding to a sexual battery case your first priority is:
   a. to calm the victim down.
   b. to initiate the BOLO.
   c. to obtain medical treatment for the victim.
   d. to locate the crime scene and secure it.

3. Interviewing a victim of sexual battery should be done:
   a. immediately at the scene.
   b. with witnesses.
   c. in private.
   d. after reading her Miranda.

4. All of the following are examples of robbery styles except:
   a. unplanned.
   b. ambush.
   c. selective.
   d. planned.

5. All dead body cases should be treated as:
   a. criminal homicides until proven otherwise.
   b. potentially dangerous due to body fluids being present.
   c. a and b above.
   d. none of the above.

6. In domestic violence cases:
   a. the officer does not have to witness the event to arrest.
   b. a battery charge is usually included.
   c. people who live together, are married or are family members are involved.
   d. all of the above.

7. DCF stands for:
   a. Department of Crisis Formulation.
   b. Division of Children's Fabrications.
   c. Department of Children and Families.
   d. none of the above.

8. Physical indicators of child abuse include all of the following except:
   a. fear of going home.
   b. burns.
   c. welts.
   d. suspicious bruises.

9. Physical indicators of child neglect include:
   a. begging for or stealing food.
   b. constant hunger.
   c. consistent lack of supervision.
   d. b and c.

10. Occupations of professionals who are required by law to report suspected child abuse include all of the following except:
    a. spiritual healer.
    b. school teacher.
    c. lifeguard.
    d. police officer.

Surveillance Techniques and Development of Information Sources

A very important part of investigation is the gathering of intelligence. One method, which is seen on many movies and television shows, is the "stake-out." This is surveillance. *Surveillance* is the covert observation of a person, group, place, or vehicle.

SCENARIO NUMBER ONE:

The Auto Theft Unit

You have been temporarily assigned to the auto theft unit. The city is experiencing a rash of car thefts from the large car lots. You are told to report Friday evening at 8:00 P.M. for briefing. At the briefing, you are given more details on the thefts and given the operational plan for the surveillance. You are assigned to a fixed post at one of the larger car lots. During the briefing you are told to remain unseen and report any observations to the senior investigator. After you are set up in a location with great visibility, you advise that you are in service at the lot. At 2:30 A.M., you observe a vehicle drive up to the lot and drop off a passenger and quickly leave. You immediately notify the senior investigator with a description of the suspect and the vehicle. He coordinates the movement of the other units. The man who got out of the car walks directly to the sports utility vehicles. As he is walking, a vehicle drives by, and he quickly drops between two vehicles. After the car passes he stands up and continues going through the line of cars. He stops at one and pulls out a metal object from his pants.

Once the suspect enters the locked car, you observe him moving around inside the vehicle. At this time, the order to move in is given. You approach the vehicle along with two back-up officers and arrest the suspect. He is turned over to the investigator. The objective of this surveillance was to detect and prevent crime.

Surveillance can be done with the assistance of electronic equipment provided that Fourth Amendment rights are not violated. The case that established this is *Katz v. United States.* In Katz, the FBI placed a listening device on the outside of a telephone booth that a bookie was using to conduct betting operations across state lines. The conviction was appealed and overturned because the agents did not have a search warrant for the phone booth.

During the interrogation of the car thief, the suspect admitted to being a member of a larger group of car thieves. He gave the investigator the names and locations that the group operates from. You are once again assigned to assist the investigators. This time you are working out of an unmarked van parked across from a salvage yard. You are in the van with an investigator who is videotaping the people coming in and out of the yard. At about 8:00 P.M., the vehicle that you observed at the car lot pulled into the yard. The driver exited the vehicle and closed the gate behind him. The investigator used a telephoto lens on a camera to photograph the driver and the vehicle. As you watched, three other vehicles came to the gate, honked their horns, and were admitted. All of the vehicles were reported stolen. Based upon this information, a search warrant was requested, and executed on the salvage yard. Several stolen vehicles were recovered, and seven people were arrested for operating a car theft ring.

The objectives of your surveillance were to locate the other known perpetrator; develop intelligence information on the theft ring; secure probable cause for a search warrant; locate, identify and arrest the members; and recover the stolen property.

The two types of surveillance you were involved in were fixed and electronic. The third type is moving. Had the suspect left the salvage yard, another investigator was available to perform a moving surveillance. This would consist of the investigator following the suspect at a distance. A successful moving surveillance utilizes several vehicles and officers.

All operations in law enforcement have some form of preparation. Surveillance is no exception. For a successful surveillance, some knowledge of the subject is an absolute necessity. First, an accurate description of the subject and some knowledge of his or her personal habits would assist you in set-up. The environment and conditions within the environment will assist in your determination of camouflage. Once you know the location, you must familiarize yourself with the area and know where the roads and streets go. One of the worst things that can happen is to follow a suspect into a dead end. You must also be aware of the danger level of the suspect in the event of a confrontation. You have to understand that if you are placing a person under surveillance, that person probably has reason to be paranoid and is looking for you. In some cases, the people who you are looking at has a counter-surveillance team that is watching you. Contingency plans are always part of the preliminary survey of the surveillance operation, as is the decision of which covert method is best to use.

Identify five objectives of surveillance:

1. _____

2. _____

3. _____

4. _____

5. _____

Describe the three types of surveillance:

1. _____

2. _____

3. _____

Identify three considerations in preparing for surveillance:

1. _____

2. _____

3. _____

Equipment is based upon the type of surveillance that is going to be done. Cameras and optical devices such as binoculars, and video recorders are used to document criminal behavior observed. Night vision scopes, wire taps, audio recorders and communication devices such as cellphones and radios are commonly used to intercept and document criminal communications.

SCENARIO NUMBER TWO:
The Contingency Plan

You are following a suspect on a foot-based moving surveillance. You are keeping a safe distance and observe him make a left turn. As you turn the corner, he is in your face.

What do you do now? Come up with three possible solutions:

1. _____

2. _____

3. _____

Prior to going on surveillance, you should have a number of contingency plans. Contingency plans include such things as what you should do when confronted by the suspect, or if the suspect drives with erratic driving patterns, what to do when a suspect boards and then disembarks from public transportation. In more technical surveillance, the suspect may have a jamming device or use other countermeasures. The purpose of countermeasures is to elude the police. The purpose of de-bugging devices is to locate eavesdropping equipment. If any of these happen, you have most likely been discovered. The two risks in surveillance are getting discovered or being eluded by the suspect.

Information Sources

Information is the most important component to any investigation. Information comes from many different sources. In the case of a crime, the victim can give you valuable information, witnesses, suspects, police officers, and people who work in public jobs can also give you information. The main thing to remember as an investigator is that people usually don't usually volunteer information—you have to ask.

SCENARIO NUMBER THREE:

The Informant

You are working in patrol. On Monday afternoon, you are dispatched to a disturbance call on the corner of Seventh and Elm. This area is best known for its drug activity, and it is considered a high-crime area. Upon your arrival, there is no disturbance. A man who you know is involved in the drug trade comes up to the car. He is acting suspiciously. He asks that you meet him in the back ally. You advise dispatch of your location and meet the individual. He has information on a large drug shipment that is coming in tonight. He provides the people involved, the vehicles, the time, quantity, and type of drugs that are being smuggled. He advises that he was just doing his civic duty and does not want anything in return. He does request that he remain anonymous.

Why would this person provide this information? What do you do?

_____

_____

_____

People provide information to the police for various reasons. Occasionally, they provide information just because it's the right thing to do. They may feel that it's their civic duty. Many times they are looking for money. It is not uncommon to pay informants for valuable information. Other times, the information could be false and purposely misleading. In the example above the man was providing good information. His motivation was not civic in nature, but business. He was eliminating the competition from a rival drug dealer. It is very common that an informant wishes to remain anonymous. Giving information on a criminal could be life-threatening. Some informants give information out of fear. They have a reason to want the suspect picked up so that they are no longer in jeopardy from him or her. Some of the informants believe themselves to be "undercover operatives" not unlike some characters in suspense movies. What motivates these informants is their vanity. A more common type of informant is one who is created out of an arrest. In an attempt to get a better deal in court, the arrested person attempts to obtain a better plea bargain by informing on people associated with his or her crime.

SCENARIO NUMBER FOUR:

The Gambling Informant

You are patrolling this same area later in the week and observe a group of four men apparently gambling. Three run away. You take the one man into custody. Since this is a low-level crime, you decide to let him go. Before you let him go, you tell him that he "owes you." A month later, you need assistance on a crime in that area.

1. What is a low-level crime?

_____

_____

2. Did you violate the law by letting this criminal go?

_____

3. Is it unethical to tell a criminal that he owes you?

_____

4. What is the benefit of having a criminal in your debt?

_____

_____

5. Does this benefit outweigh the possible negative effects of this "deal"?

_____

You contact him and receive valuable information on the case and he advises you that "we're even." When a person is guilty of a crime, sometimes their conscience bothers them. A person who is repentant may provide excellent information on his or her crimes or the crimes of others. Jilted girlfriends and wives inform on their boyfriends or husbands to get even.

As a good patrol officer, you know your zone. You know the people who live and work there. When you eat lunch, you take time to talk to the restaurant owners, and you visit the merchants and business people who work in your zone. When there is trouble, they are comfortable talking to you. They have gotten to know you as a person who happens to be a cop. Your day-to-day contacts will pay off in valuable information that will help you solve crimes. As stated earlier, if you don't ask they won't tell you. If they don't know or trust you, they are less likely to tell you things.

Identify five motivational factors that may cause a person to become an informant:

1. _____

2. _____

3. _____

4. _____

5. _____

Every time an informant provides information, he or she is taking a risk. The law enforcement officer should never forget this. If you use an informant, you should not be careless, and you should treat the informant with consideration. As a police officer, your word is your bond. Never promise things that you can't deliver on. Always fulfill your promises. Always remember that the informant may have ulterior motives and should not be trusted 100 percent. Never allow the informant to take charge of even a small part of the investigation. All information must be evaluated. An informant who doesn't provide credible information is worthless. If you are developing probable cause based upon an informant's information, you must be absolutely positive as to the information.

On occasion, you will encounter a juvenile with information. You should be very careful in dealing with juveniles. They are young and sometimes don't realize the danger involved. If a juvenile is to be used, his or her parents must provide permission.

CROSSWORD PUZZLE

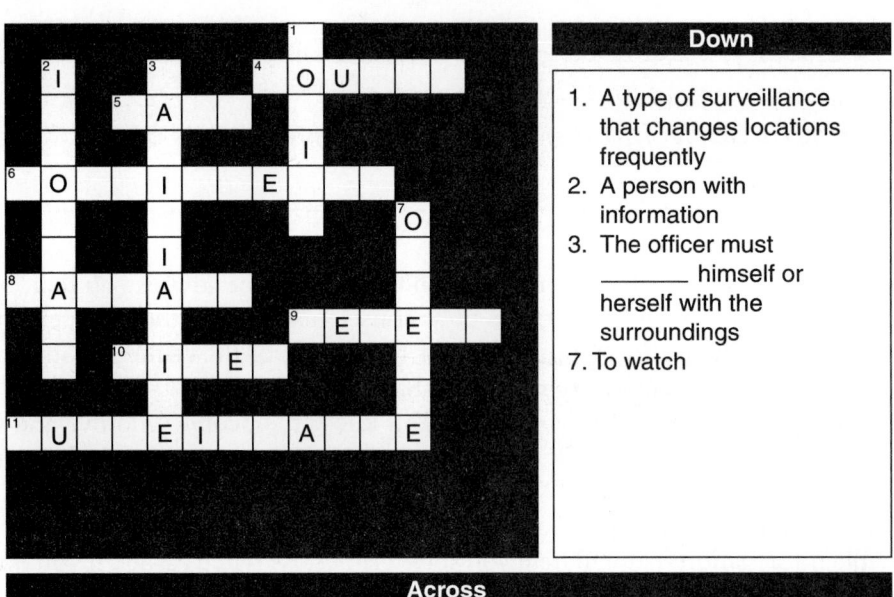

Down

1. A type of surveillance that changes locations frequently
2. A person with information
3. The officer must _____ himself or herself with the surroundings
7. To watch

Across

4. This Amendment involves search and seizure
5. _____ vs. *United States* involved the Fourth Amendment
6. A plan to use if things go wrong
8. A search _____ allows officers to legally enter private property in order to obtain evidence
9. To discover
10. A _____ post surveillance is one that does not move
11. Covert observations of suspects

SUMMARY

In this chapter, we defined surveillance and identified the legal precedence of using electronic surveillance. We reviewed the objectives of surveillance. We discussed the operational plan, which is used prior to conducting surveillance, and identified the three types of surveillance. Special considerations in the preparation of surveillance were presented, as was the need for a preliminary survey. The types of equipment used in surveillance and situations that indicate that the suspect has discovered you were also identified. The common risks involved in surveillance were also described.

The people who commonly provide information to the police were identified, as were the types and motivations of informants. The concept of community policing and its relationship to the gathering of information was discussed. The rules regarding treatment of informants were identified, as was the importance of the evaluating informant information when developing probable cause. Finally, the use of juveniles as informants was discussed.

Test Your Knowledge

1. _____ is known as a discreet observation of a person, group, place, or vehicle
   a. Countermeasures
   b. Eavesdropping
   c. Surveillance
   d. Spying

2. In the case of _____ v. *United States,* electronic surveillance came into question.
   a. *Katz*
   b. *Dogz*
   c. *Mize*
   d. *Ratz*

3. All of the following are examples of objectives of surveillance except:
   a. detecting and preventing crime.
   b. locating and recovering stolen property.
   c. developing counter surveillance.
   d. obtaining information to use in interrogations.

4. All of the following are examples of different types of surveillance except:
   a. fixed.
   b. moving.
   c. rotational.
   d. electronic.

5. All of the following are examples of surveillance equipment except:
   a. optical devices.
   b. television.
   c. wiretap devices.
   d. communication devices.

6. Common risks involved in surveillance include:
   a. car crashes.
   b. being discovered.
   c. being eluded by the suspect.
   d. b and c.

7. Types of informants include all of the following except:
   a. amateur.
   b. rival.
   c. self-aggrandizing.
   d. false.

8. Motivational factors which may cause an individual to become an informant include all of the following except:
   a. insanity.
   b. fear.
   c. jealousy.
   d. revenge.

9. The rules regarding the treatment of informants include:
   a. informant should be treated considerately.
   b. investigator should allow the informant to take charge.
   c. investigator should fulfill all ethical promises which have been made.
   d. a and c.

10. Difficulties involved in the using of juveniles as informants include:
    a. possible compromising situations.
    b. parental permission is required.
    c. it is illegal to use juveniles.
    d. a and b.

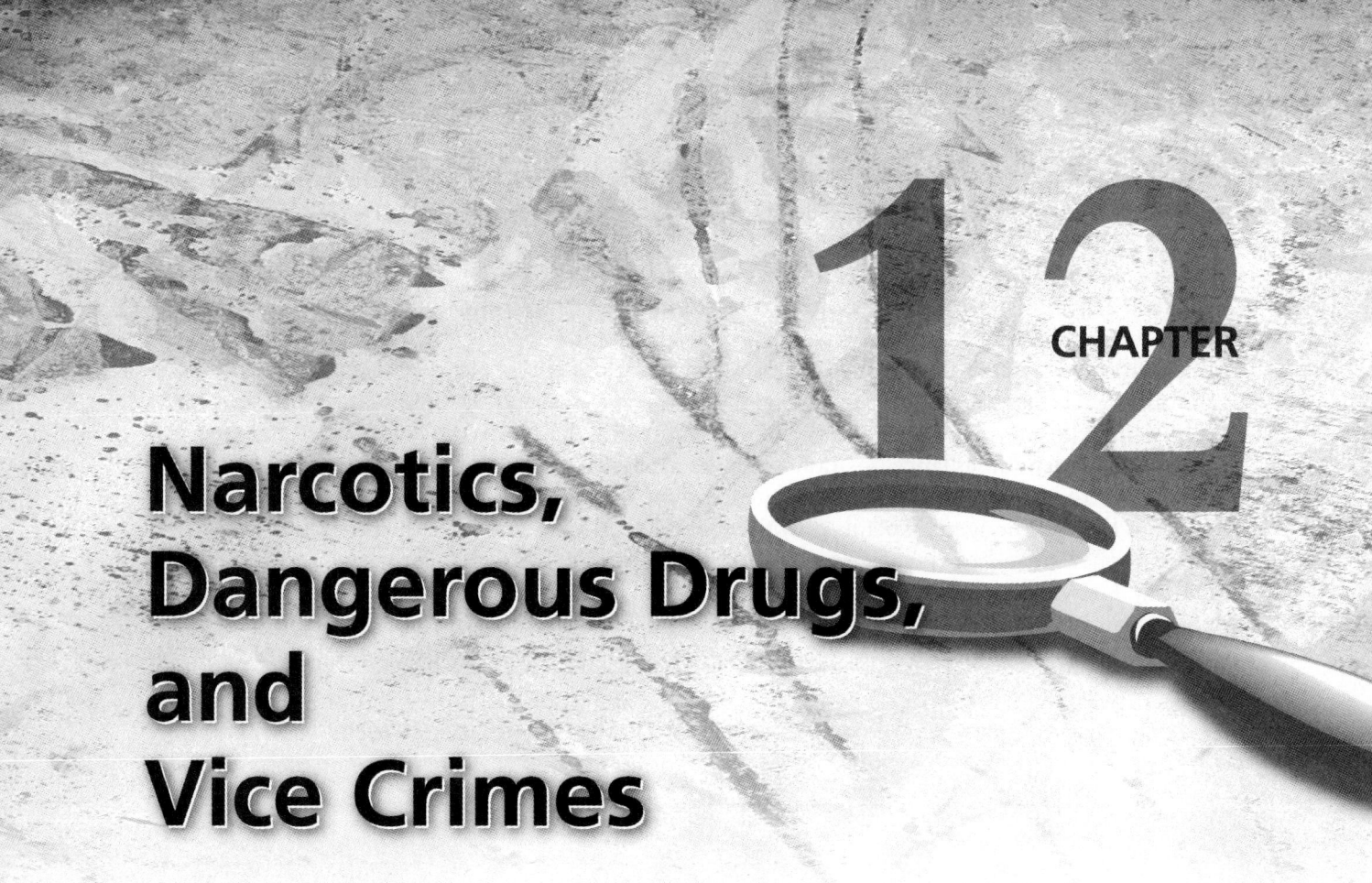

Narcotics, Dangerous Drugs, and Vice Crimes

Drug-related crime is something that will be with us as long as people choose to use illegal and dangerous drugs. Drug-related activity is normally not done in the open and is often not reported. People involved with or addicted to drugs are active participants in the crimes associated with drugs and are not likely to turn in their dealer. If their dealer gets locked up, they must go elsewhere to get their drugs. The family and friends of the drug users tend to protect them or are ashamed of their addiction and choose not to be involved.

SCENARIO NUMBER ONE:

The Drug Unit

You are temporarily assigned to work with the undercover drug unit. The unit sergeant briefs you about undercover operations in general and your duties while assigned to the unit. The sergeant brings you into the evidence room to show you a collection of drug paraphernalia. There are syringes of different types and sizes, scales for weighing drugs, small plastic baggies, an assortment of pipes, spoons used to prepare heroin, medicine droppers, rolling papers, razor blades with glass slabs for cutting cocaine and aluminum cans, which are bent and have burn marks in the center and are used for smoking crack. He advises you that the informants are comprised of citizens and criminals. Your first duty is to answer the tip line and screen out the calls that are productive. After answering the phone for some time, you are given a tip by a person who sounds sincere. A woman called to report her son's activity in a gang that is known for dealing drugs. She warned her son to stay away from them, but he refuses. She followed him on several occasions and provided the address where they are making crack along with the names of the other members of the gang. As you pass this along to the undercover agents, they advise that they are working this group already and ask you to come along on their operation. As you are riding with one of the agents, he describes the mobile surveillance that you and he are about to begin. You are following one of the gang members to gather intelligence on his contacts. At the end of the day, you have six addresses and four vehicle tags to run. This operation will provide the names of some of the contacts outside of the gang who may be supporting them with supplies. The following day you are assigned to a fixed or stationary surveillance position with two agents who are in an apartment across the street from where the gang operates. In the apartment are several electronic devices and cameras with telephoto lenses. The agent explains how the wiretap works. You observe the other agent with a set of headphones on and a large tape recorder operating. It was apparent that the agent was intercepting a call. He was making a notation on a log sheet and listening intently. The agent explained how important it is to keep detailed and accurate records. These cases have a high probability of going to trial, as the penalties for dealing drugs are high. This is especially true in federal court.

Identify three reasons why drug activity is normally not reported:

1. _____

2. _____

3. _____

List three methods used in narcotics investigations:

1. _____

2. _____

3. _____

Identify six types of paraphernalia:

1. _____

2. _____

3. _____

4. _____

5. _____

6. _____

Drug trafficking is big business. There are three basic ways that drugs are produced.

1. Smuggling is the oldest and most common method. Smugglers bring drugs into the country by vehicles and on individual people who are contracted by the smuggler. People who carry drugs on or inside their bodies for pay are known as "mules." They are often intercepted at airports and detained until the evidence is passed. Drugs can be hidden in vehicles with special compartments. Some dwellings are also equipped with hidden spaces for drug storage. Large-scale smugglers use ships and even commercial airplanes to transport their supply.

2. The next source of illicit drugs comes from diversion or hijacking pharmaceutical trucks.

3. The final source is the clandestine laboratory. The word laboratory brings to mind a scientific lab you may have seen on television. These labs have very little in common with scientific labs. There is little or no quality control, the chemicals are treated carelessly and pose a great hazard to agents who are executing search warrants. Several of these labs have blown up. These labs produce methamphetamine, which is commonly known as crank, speed, or ice. A crack lab is much less dangerous and is often produced in the dealer's kitchen. The powder form of cocaine is transformed into crack by a simple process involving household chemicals and ingredients.

List three sources of drug traffic in the United States:

1. _____

2. _____

3. _____

SCENARIO NUMBER TWO:

The Search Warrant

After your surveillance, the agents approached the court for a search warrant. The drug squad met at 3:00 A.M. to prepare for a 4:30 A.M. search warrant execution. The sergeant had the lead agent present the briefing. The SWAT team was present and went over the operational aspects of the entry and security of the scene. At 4:30, the search warrant was executed, and the scene was secured. Seven people were asleep in the house at the time of the execution. The first thing the SWAT team did was to secure all of the people in the house. The agents then moved in to seize the contraband and formally arrest the suspects. You were tasked to mark and package the evidence. Prior to collecting the drugs, you put rubber gloves on for protection. You carefully weighed and counted the drugs prior to sealing them in plastic bags with evidence tape and filled out the chain-of-custody forms on each article. You filled the lab analysis form prior to turning them in to the evidence custodian. That afternoon, the warrant was returned to the court as served. A well-executed raid is conducted safely. A good search results in evidence being seized, and suspects being apprehended and successfully prosecuted in court.

Identify three common areas for drug concealment:

1. _____

2. _____

3. _____

List the three principle considerations of a properly planned and executed search warrant or raid:

1. _____

2. _____

3. _____

Identify three major components of handling narcotics evidence:

1. _____

2. _____

3. _____

VICE CRIMES

The term vice brings to mind a character flaw, habit, or even an addiction. Using tobacco products, drinking alcoholic beverages, and gambling are all considered legal vices. All three are highly regulated by the government. Alcohol is not sold on Sundays in some jurisdictions. Pornography and prostitution have been around since people began to live together in civilized groups. These types of crimes are commonly known as *victimless crimes*. A victimless crime is an offense that violates the moral standard of a community and one in which the victim actively participates. This is based upon a typical model of crime that involves a criminal and his victim. These types of crimes involve both the *victim* (customer) and the *perpetrator* (supplier) in the commission of the act.

SCENARIO NUMBER THREE:

The Vice Unit

You are assigned to the vice unit to assist in a prostitution sting operation. Two female officers are dressed in civilian clothes and placed on street corners that are frequented by prostitutes. The officers are wired with hidden microphones. You are in a van parked on the corner observing the operation and taping the conversation. A vehicle approaches the undercover officer and asks for sex for twenty dollars. The female officer gives the prearranged signal that probable cause for arrest is made.

Two other officers approach the vehicle and arrest the suspect. His vehicle is removed from the area, and he is secured and charged with assignation of prostitution.

This is an example of a tactical operation based upon numerous complaints from citizens.

Did the undercover officer entrap the suspect? Why or Why not?

_____

_____

_____

Entrapment involves law enforcement inducing or causing a suspect to commit a crime so that the officer may then arrest the suspect.

Vice crimes are investigated through the gathering of intelligence, the use of informants, and surveillance. The participants don't complain to the police. Information normally comes from other sources such as angry neighbors who are tired of prostitutes working their neighborhood. Vice crimes are worked by using tactical methods such as the prostitute sting above or by strategic planning which could result in the changing of laws to combat a problem. Strategic intelligence identifies areas of concern for police enforcement, training and curriculum in police academies, as well as governmental entities. Strategic intelligence is also used to educate the public in crime prevention. To alleviate a problem with prostitutes and intoxicated patrons around adult entertainment establishments, the government proposed a law banning public nudity. This, in effect, shut down the adult entertainment business and solved the initial problem. Laws can be changed and modified to combat organized crime at the state level as well.

Identify three types of "victimless" crimes:

1. _____

2. _____

3. _____

List the three primary methods used when investigating vice activity:

1. _____

2. _____

3. _____

Identify three types of strategic intelligence:

1. _____

2. _____

3. _____

Tactical intelligence is information that provides evidence of a crime. This was the case when you assisted in the surveillance at the drug house. The surveillance provided information that was substantive and was helpful in prosecuting the case. The information also helped identify criminals and showed relationships that indicated a conspiracy. Tactical intelligence allows officers to focus upon a specific area of criminal activity. The focus of the auto theft investigation included information collection on the modus operandi as well as identifying all of the suspects.

Identify three types of tactical intelligence:

1. _____

2. _____

3. _____

CROSSWORD PUZZLE

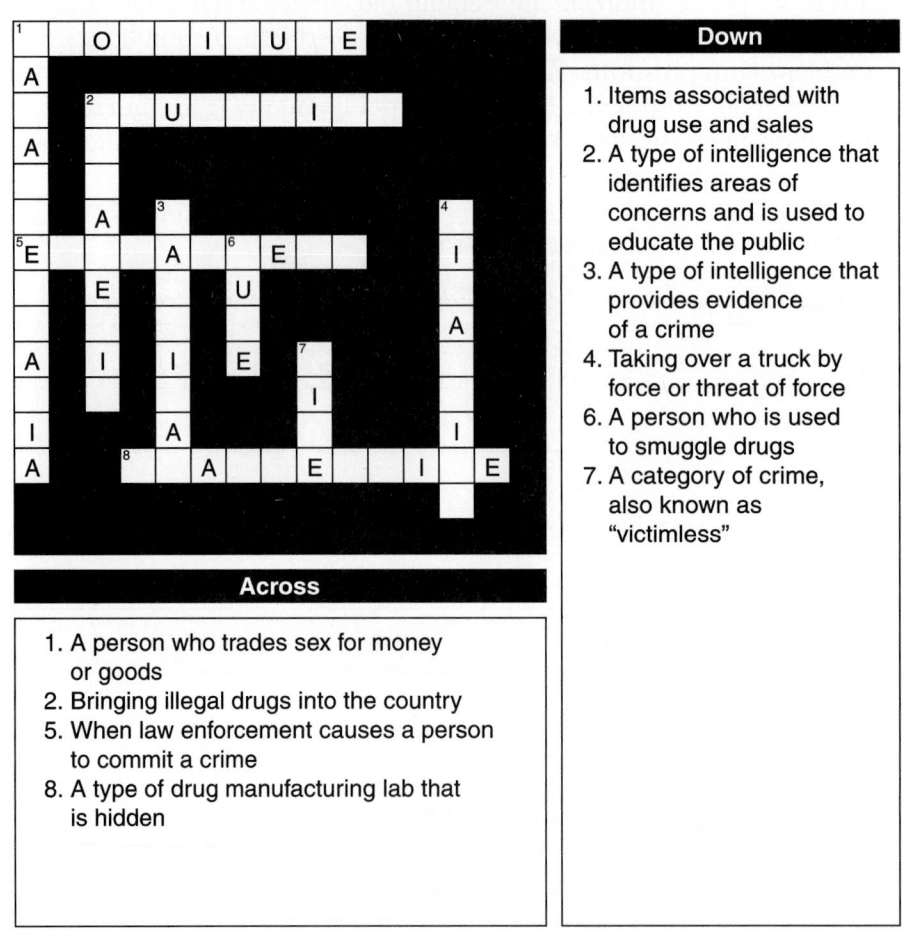

Down

1. Items associated with drug use and sales
2. A type of intelligence that identifies areas of concerns and is used to educate the public
3. A type of intelligence that provides evidence of a crime
4. Taking over a truck by force or threat of force
6. A person who is used to smuggle drugs
7. A category of crime, also known as "victimless"

Across

1. A person who trades sex for money or goods
2. Bringing illegal drugs into the country
5. When law enforcement causes a person to commit a crime
8. A type of drug manufacturing lab that is hidden

SUMMARY

In this chapter, we listed common reasons why drug activity is not normally reported and the methods used in narcotics investigations. We discussed the different types of paraphernalia and sources of illicit drug traffic in the United States. Later, we identified the major components of handling narcotic evidence as well as the common ways they are transported and concealed. The steps taken after a search warrant for drugs were discussed, as were the principle considerations of a properly planned and conducted search warrant or raid. Victimless crimes were listed as were primary methods used to investigate vice activity. The chapter concluded with examples of the use of strategic and tactical intelligence and the definition of entrapment.

Test Your Knowledge

1. All of the following are examples of why drug activity is rarely reported except:
   a. the victim of the dealer is a party to the crime.
   b. there are no victims.
   c. the victim must cooperate with the dealer to preserve the source of the supply.
   d. relatives and friends of users are protective, ashamed, and do not want to get involved.

2. Common methods used in narcotics investigations include:
   a. undercover operations.
   b. overt operations.
   c. informants.
   d. a and c.

3. Types of paraphernalia used in illegal drug activities include all of the following except:
   a. needles.
   b. scales.
   c. forks.
   d. spoons.

4. Sources of illicit drug traffic include:
   a. smuggling.
   b. diversion.
   c. laboratories.
   d. all the above.

5. Major components of handling narcotic evidence include:
   a. collection.
   b. return.
   c. counting and weighing.
   d. transmission to lab.

6. Common methods of transporting drugs include:
   a. vehicles.
   b. on persons.
   c. on animals.
   d. a and b.

7. Common areas for drug concealment include all of the following except:
   a. body cavities.
   b. premises (dwellings).
   c. in plain view.
   d. vehicles.

8. Steps taken after obtaining a search warrant for drugs include:
   a. execute warrant.
   b. release persons.
   c. make arrests.
   d. a and c.

9. All of the following are examples of victimless crimes except:
   a. robbery.
   b. gambling.
   c. prostitution.
   d. pornography.

10. The primary methods used when investigating vice activity include:
    a. intelligence.
    b. informants.
    c. traffic analysis.
    d. a and b.

13 CHAPTER

Bombs/Explosive Violations Organized Crime Familiarization and Terrorists

Hollywood has had a field day with the concept of organized crime. Literally hundreds of films have depicted Mafia hitmen and gangsters. Some Italian Americans have actively protested the stereotyping that they believe these movies promote. The average police officer is not going to encounter Hollywood-type gangsters on a daily basis. However, organized crime does indeed exist. It has a very specific structure that has been described repeatedly in the movies that have been produced on the topic. The structure is based upon a Mafia model that came to this country from Sicily. Because of this, the hierarchical titles are in Italian. The head of the family is known as the Don and the chain of command runs from him through lower-level supervisors to the soldiers or *caporegimas*.

Organized crime has both illegal criminal enterprises as well as legitimate businesses. Many times the legitimate businesses are used to launder monies gained illegally. This mixture provides the organization with an ongoing profit continuity, which is unaffected by personnel in the organization. A small restaurant may appear to have few customers but show a large profit. Organized crime is divided into strict territories. The organizations tend to operate a monopoly in the area that they control. Because of the enormous amounts of money generated by these organizations, and the layers of insulation between the soldiers and the top personnel, the leaders enjoy a state of relative immunity from being arrested or prosecuted.

SCENARIO NUMBER ONE:
The Hijacking

You are working as a patrol officer. You are dispatched to a hijacking of a semi-tractor-trailer that was full of clothing bound for a major department store. As you are questioning the driver, you get the feeling that he does not want to cooperate fully in the investigation. His answers to your questions are vague, and he appears to be frightened. When you are finished with your report, you realize that the victim was not really helpful at all. This case may have been orchestrated by organized crime and the driver warned not to cooperate.

The cost of this type of crime is passed on to consumers in the form of higher prices. Public servants such as judges are corrupted by organized crime through bribery or extortion. The amount of crime that is associated with the distribution and sale of drugs on the street is well documented. Organized crime is behind a great deal of street crime. Gambling is acceptable in most jurisdictions in some form such as lottery or even bingo. People get addicted to gambling and resort to loan sharks who charge enormous interest. When they can't pay the loan shark they steal from their employers or are forced into criminal activity such as transporting narcotics or white-collar crime. Being in debt to criminals can result in great bodily injury or even death. The sex trade is another big business that has a huge income. Organized crime can be found involved in all aspects of the sex industry including pornography, adult entertainment establishments, and prostitution.

Identify three characteristics exhibited in organized crime:

1. _____

2. _____

3. _____

List the impact organized crime activity has on the public:

1. _____

2. _____

3. _____

Identify six illicit activities with which organized crime is associated:

1. _____

2. _____

3. _____

4. _____

5. _____

6. _____

Some organized crime operations include fencing stolen property, chop shops, and car theft rings, as well as stolen credit card operations. Illegal lottery games known as "numbers" are a constant in lower economic communities. Two of the most common "legitimate" businesses operated by organized crime are vending machine companies and trash collection.

SCENARIO NUMBER TWO:

The County City Investigative Unit

You are temporarily assigned to the County City Investigation Unit. This unit is comprised of officers from different cities within the county and is used to combat vice and organized crime activities. You have been tasked to drive a van with an assortment of officers on a raid. The raid is on a major supplier of drugs to the local area. Upon your arrival, the officers jump out of the van and execute a search warrant. At the end of the night four people were arrested and over $100,000 in cash was seized as well as four kilograms of cocaine. One of the agents advised that these people will be charged in federal court and the house is going to be forfeited as well.

One of the best tools law enforcement has in combating organized crime is the ability to go after ill-got gains. Houses, cars, boats, planes, and anything that can be tied to the illegal operation are subject to forfeiture. By combining resources, agencies share intelligence and can concentrate their efforts.

TERRORISM

Many cities are preparing for possible terrorist attacks involving chemical and biological agents. There have been several movies involving outbreaks of biological agents such as the Ebola virus. Terrorists kidnap people, and blackmail and intimidate people through well-founded fear. A terrorist does not hesitate in killing people to make a point. Terrorists fund their activities by thefts and bank robberies. Political terrorists may explode a bomb in a crowded subway in order to make a political statement. One type of terrorist creates urban disturbances such as burning up a building in order to get the attention of the landlord. After a landlord loses one building, he or she may rethink paying for protection from the criminals. Terrorists use violence for persuasion. They select their targets based upon their perceived value for propaganda. The people who are targeted have done nothing to deserve the attack. Attacking people who are not prepared provides the greatest impact with the least amount of risk to the terrorists. In the World Trade Center bombing, surprise overcame countermeasures. The Federal Building in Oklahoma was not designed to prevent the attack which took place. After the fact, federal agencies put preventive measures in place so that vehicles are not able to approach buildings as closely as was done in Oklahoma. The primary weapon of the terrorist is fear. Shock factor and the fact that children and women are targeted equally with men make the attack more horrific and therefore more effective. After an attack, it is normal for the terrorists to take responsibility for the act and to provide propaganda to justify their actions. Members of the terrorist organization are extremely loyal; some are religious fanatics who sacrifice their own lives for the cause.

Today hundreds of terrorist organizations operate around the world. The Ku Klux Klan is a terrorist organization that was formed after the U.S. Civil War in order to terrorize the newly freed slaves. Skin Heads, Neo-Nazis, and the Aryan Nation are closely related to the KKK and share white supremacist views. President Bill Clinton released Puerto Rican terrorists from prison in a controversial pardon. This group was responsible for a number of bombings and terrorist acts. Their motivation was the independence of Puerto Rico. Cuban terrorists also have been active for their causes. The Jewish Defense League and the Palestinian Liberation Organization both have their own agendas and retaliate over these issues. Bombings in Israel and Palestine are all too common.

List five criminal activities used by terrorists:

1. _____

2. _____

3. _____

4. _____

5. _____

Identify three types of terrorism:

1. _____

2. _____

3. _____

List three characteristics of terrorism:

1. _____

2. _____

3. _____

Name six domestic and international terrorist groups:

1. _____

2. _____

3. _____

4. _____

5. _____

6. _____

BOMBS/EXPLOSIVES

Everyone has seen the results of bombs, both military and homemade. Bombs are indiscriminate and devastating devices. According to the Florida Department of Law Enforcement, a bomb is "any chemical compound, mixture or device whose primary or common purpose is to function by explosion with substantially instantaneous release of gas and heat." Bombs are used to destroy property, kill and maim people, and to intimidate people through fear.

SCENARIO NUMBER THREE:

The Mail Box

You are in routine patrol. You are dispatched to 111 Oak Avenue in reference to criminal mischief. Upon your arrival, you observe the remains of a mailbox by the street. All that remains intact is the post to which the mailbox was attached. On the ground next to pieces of the mailbox are the remains of a one-liter plastic bottle. The owner advises that he heard a car drive up and then an explosion. He said that he is a teacher and that some of his students were unhappy with their mid-term grades. He could not identify the suspects. You collected the evidence and submitted them for processing and finished your report.

1. Is this a federal offense?

_____

_____

2. Do you notify the Federal Bureau of Investigation?

_____

_____

3. Are you required to contact the Postal Inspectors Office?

_____

_____

4. Would this qualify as a "hate" crime?

_____

_____

5. Based upon the evidence, what type of device was used to destroy the mailbox?

_____

_____

Although there are federal laws that protect the United States Mail, criminal mischief such as the destroying of a mailbox does not normally apply. The officer would normally take a criminal mischief report in this case, and it would be turned over to the department investigators. The fact that it was a soda bottle bomb rather than standard fireworks, or the more common destruction by a baseball bat, would give the police concern. This type of device is dangerous, and felony charges could easily be levied upon the perpetrators. Although his students might not like him, a teacher is not normally considered to be the victim of a hate crime because of his occupation.

There are three types of explosions.

1. Mechanical explosions are caused by a device that contains an explosive material. When the device functions, the material explodes.

2. Chemical explosions are caused by mixing two chemicals, which when mixed cause an explosion. In the example above, the mailbox was blown up by a seltzer bottle bomb. This bomb is made by mixing common household chemicals in a plastic bottle. The bomb used in Oklahoma was made predominantly of fertilizer.

3. A nuclear bomb uses radioactive materials and is extremely complex.

SCENARIO NUMBER FOUR:
The Bomb Threat

The probation and parole department has called in a suspicious case left in the lobby. As you are aware, probation and parole receive numerous bomb threats every year. You respond to their office and inquire as to the specifics. In the lobby is an attaché case, which no one can identify. You instruct all personnel to evacuate the building and advise the department over the telephone. You have turned off your radio. If the device has a transmitter, your radio can detonate it. You know not to touch the case or place any metal object near it. Some bombs have mercury switches that will detonate the device if moved. The bomb squad arrives and sends in a small robotic device with a water cannon. The device activates the water cannon and the attaché explodes open and a stack of papers fly all over the office.

Anyone can construct an effective bomb. If a bomb is detonated, much of the evidence is destroyed. Much of the time, there are no witnesses. The indiscriminate devastation caused by a bomb creates terror in people and is a very effective tool of the terrorist. Random bombings make people afraid and apprehensive. When the target is an international jetliner, people become fearful of flying. In both these instances, the terrorist has completed his or her objective. The terrorist's act is on the mind of the people.

Identify the three types of explosions:

1. _____

2. _____

3. _____

List the precautions to follow when a suspected bomb is found:

1. _____

2. _____

3. _____

4. _____

Bombing incidents call for people who are specially trained and skilled in their individual areas. When a bombing or bomb threat is reported, it is important that personnel with *protective* skills are present. These people may be medical personnel who set up a triage to handle wounded victims. They may be search and rescue personnel who will work through the rubble looking for survivors. Police officers who can deal with and control frightened or excited persons and make decisions under stress are absolutely necessary. People with *technical* skills, which are used in the defusing of a bomb or the analysis of the suspected device, are necessary. Highly skilled *investigators* are needed to piece the scene back together, interview victims, analyze evidence and identify suspects.

SCENARIO NUMBER FIVE:
The Middle School

You are called to the middle school in reference to a bomb threat. When you arrive, the school has evacuated the students to the perimeter of the school property. The principal requests that the school be searched. You advise her that the most effective method is the *team* search. This search will take a great deal of time and manpower and requires the cooperation of the people who work in the school. As you look around the school, you begin to realize that a bomb could be anywhere, and it could be disguised as *anything*. The team search pairs together police officers and people who work at the place where the threat has been called in. The teams go the entire scene looking at everything. If an object such as a potted plant is observed in the hall, the person who works there could advise if it has been there or if it is new. You search every inch of the school and find nothing. Even after a thorough search, a bomb could still be present. In most instances a student called in the threat.

If this was not a hoax, and an explosion occurred, than the investigators working on the bomb scene would attempt to ascertain if the explosion was an accident or intentional. Investigators must be able to determine *how* the explosion occurred, *what* was used to cause the explosion, and *why*. The investigators will attempt to identify the suspect and collect evidence that will link the suspect to the scene.

SCENARIO NUMBER SIX:
The Post Office

You are called to the post office in reference to a possible explosive device that was discovered in the mail. Your first consideration is how you are going to respond to this call. Does this require lights and sirens? Once you make the determination of how to make your *initial response,* you proceed to the post office. Upon your arrival, the postal inspector greets you. You have turned off your radio. Two other officers join you at the post office. Across the street is the probation and parole office. You request that one of the officers go to the probation and parole office to *establish a command post and coordinate communication.* No radios will be used. You begin the basic evacuation process and clear the building. You request that traffic units establish a perimeter and seal off the area from traffic. The postal inspector brings you to the suspected ticking package. You *recognize* this package as being a possible *explosive or incendiary device* as it is emitting a loud ticking sound. You *initiate a search* for any other objects with the inspector. Nothing else is found. All of the packages and mail is moved to another location for *damage control.* The bomb squad arrives, and the suspected device is shot by the water cannon from the robotic device. Prior to the detonation, you ensure that the perimeter is expanded and further evacuated. The package is detonated and a clock and wrapping paper is discovered. After the scene is returned to the post office, you now *record and report* the event.

On some occasions a bomb threat is written. The note must be preserved by placing it in an envelope without folding and with minimal handling. This evidence must be submitted for processing by the laboratory. Once the note is collected, a supervisor must be notified.

The majority of bomb threats are telephonic. The operators of the establishments must be trained on how to deal with a bomb threat. Part of the training should include techniques to keep the caller on the line. If possible, a recording device should be made available to record the suspect if possible. The call should be traced if possible. The operator should make note of the time the call was received and terminated as well as the exact words that were spoken by the suspect. The operator must notify the authorities as soon as possible. Some of the information, which the operator should be attempting to obtain from the suspect, should include when the bomb is to explode, where, what kind of device it is, what it is made of, and what it looks like. If the suspect will advise why the device was placed, the operator should make note of this explanation. On occasion the caller may even identify himself or herself if asked. If this caller represents an organization, it is important to make note of this.

Identify three basic skill requirements for handling bomb/explosive incidents:

1. _____

2. _____

3. _____

List three responsibilities of the patrol officer when handling bomb/explosive situations:

1. _____

2. _____

3. _____

Identify three procedures for handling a bomb threat made by telephone:

1. _____

2. _____

3. _____

List three types of information that should be obtained from a caller making a bomb threat:

1. _____

2. _____

3. _____

It is extremely important that the operator or person receiving the call make special note of the gender, race, age, tone of voice, and accent of the caller. The operator should try to remember if the voice is familiar. Any background noise can be helpful in identifying the location of the caller. Any threats made by the caller indicating the nature of the call must be noted. The caller may be motivated by politics or hate. The caller may mention race, nationality or religion.

SUMMARY

In this final chapter, we listed the four basic characteristics exhibited in organized crime operations. The impact that organized crime activity has on the public and the illicit activities with which organized crime is associated were also identified. The methods used to enhance efforts to combat organized crime were also listed.

Various criminal activities used by terrorists were identified next, as were the various types of terrorism. The different characteristics of terrorism were listed, as were the various domestic and international terrorist organizations.

The definition and purpose of bombs was discussed, as were the types of explosions. Precautions to follow when a suspected bomb is found were identified, as were skill requirements involved

CROSSWORD PUZZLE

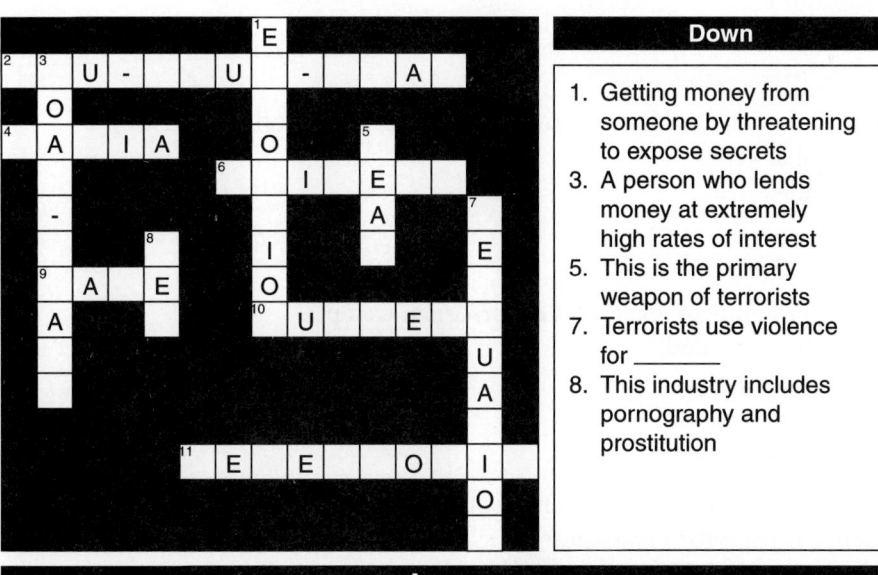

Down

1. Getting money from someone by threatening to expose secrets
3. A person who lends money at extremely high rates of interest
5. This is the primary weapon of terrorists
7. Terrorists use violence for _____
8. This industry includes pornography and prostitution

Across

2. An American terrorist organization founded after slavery was abolished
4. The organization which the *Godfather* movie was about
6. A person who gives government officials money for favors is guilty of this
9. A type of crime which targets people because of their race or religious beliefs
10. An illegal lottery
11. The most common method of transmitting a bomb threat

in handling bomb and explosive incidents. The concept of the team search was explained, as were the objectives of the bomb scene investigators. The duties of the patrol officer when handling bomb/explosive situations were identified, as were the procedures for handling a bomb threat by letter and telephone. The information that an operator should obtain from a caller making a bomb threat was listed, as were observations that are helpful in identifying a suspect who makes the call.

Test Your Knowledge

1. All of the following are characteristics exhibited in organized crime operations except:
   a. hierarchical structure.
   b. nonprofit continuity.
   c. monopoly.
   d. relative immunity.

2. The impact organized crime has on the public include:
   a. public corruption.
   b. street crime.
   c. increases in social security.
   d. a and b.

3. All of the following are examples of activities that organized crime are associated with except:
   a. gambling.
   b. prostitution.
   c. trash collection.
   d. food service.

4. Criminal activities used by terrorists include all of the following except:
   a. white-collar crime.
   b. kidnapping.
   c. theft.
   d. bank robbery.

5. All of the following are examples of terrorism except:
   a. politically motivated.
   b. rural disturbances.
   c. urban disturbances.
   d. criminal activities.

6. The different characteristics of terrorism include:
   a. violence is used for persuasion.
   b. targets are selected for propaganda.
   c. attacks are provoked.
   d. a and b.

7. All of the following are domestic and international terrorist organizations except:
   a. Aryan Nation.
   b. Provisional ERA.
   c. Jewish Defense League.
   d. Palestinian Liberation Organization.

8. Types of explosives include:
   a. mechanical.
   b. electronic.
   c. chemical.
   d. a and c.

9. Responsibilities of the patrol officer when handling bombs and explosives include all of the following except:
   a. establish a command post.
   b. conduct basic evacuation procedures.
   c. secure and remove the device.
   d. recognition of explosive and incendiary device.

10. Information which should be obtained from a caller making a bomb threat include all of the following except:
    a. where the bomb is located.
    b. when is the bomb going to explode.
    c. what kind of bomb is it.
    d. where did the bomb come from.

BIBLIOGRAPHY

The following resources are recommended for further reading:

Bennett, Wayne W., and Karen M. Hess. 1998. *Criminal Investigation*. 5th ed. California: Wadsworth Publishing Company.

Gilbert, James N. 2001. *Criminal Investigation*. 5th ed. New Jersey: Prentice-Hall, Inc.

Federal Bureau of Investigations, Bulletins and Publications. http://www.fbi.gov/

Florida Department of Law Enforcement. 1999. *Basic Recruit Training Program for Police and Corrections*.

United States Army FM 19-20 (Criminal Investigations)
http://www.adtdl.army.mil/cgi-bin/atdl.dll/fm/19-20/toc.htm

INDEX